Reflections on Bishop Xaverio Johnsai MUNYONGANI: When God called ... his job here was done

... contributing testimonies from 3 Zimbabwean Catholic priests and 15 members of the laity

Joseph Foroma

Copyright © 2021 Joseph Foroma.

Reflections on Bishop Xaverio Johnsai MUNYONGANI

ISBN: 978-1-77920-511-7

First Printed in 2021

All rights reserved. No part of this publication may be reproduced, distributed, or transmitted in any form or by any means, including photocopying, recording or other electronic or mechanical methods, without the prior written permission of the publishers. This book may not be lent, resold, hired out or otherwise disposed of by way of trade in any form, binding or cover other than that in which it is published, without the prior consent of the publishers.

Layouts by Daniel Mutendi of DanTs Media Publishing

Front and back cover designs by Ishevanhu Zengeya

DEDICATION

In memory of the late Bishop Xaverio Johnsai Munyongani, Rest In Peace

Nearer, My God, to Thee Nearer to Thee! E'en though it be a cross

Nearer, my God, to Thee, nearer to Thee! E'en though it be a cross that raiseth me,
Still all my song shall be, nearer, my God, to Thee.

Though like the wanderer, the sun gone down,
Darkness be over me, my rest a stone;
Yet in my dreams I'd be nearer, my God, to Thee.

There let the way appear, steps unto Heav'n;
All that Thou sendest me, in mercy giv'n;
Angels to beckon me nearer, my God, to Thee.

Then, with my waking thoughts bright with Thy praise,
Out of my stony griefs Bethel I'll raise;
So by my woes to be nearer, my God, to Thee.

Or, if on joyful wing cleaving the sky,
Sun, moon, and stars forgot, upward I'll fly,
Still all my song shall be, nearer, my God, to Thee.

There in my Father's home, safe and at rest,
There in my Saviour's love, perfectly blest;
Age after age to be nearer, my God, to Thee.
(Sarah Flower Adams, 1805 - 1848)

"Yesterday you brought me a nice satisfaction. In the vineyard, Ali said to me: 'So, one can really tell you're beginning to know how to prune.' To do it well you have to look beyond the branch that's apparently dead. You have to see the invisible fruit, still to come. This fruit is for everyone, and so we must work together."

Monastic Series: Number Thirty-Seven

Born from the Gaze of God: The Tibhirine Journal of a Martyr Monk (1993-1996), Christophe Lebreton, OCSO. Translated by Mette Louise Nygård and Edith Scholl, OCSO

© 2014 by Order of Saint Benedict, Collegeville, Minnesota. Used with permission.

FOREWORD

It is with great joy that we, the Catholic bishops of Zimbabwe provide the foreword to this book titled "When God called – his job here was done" which reflects on the life and work of the late Bishop Xaverio Johnsai Munyongani. Starting out from humble origins at his rural home near Mutero in Gutu, God called him to the priesthood from which he never looked back or wavered. His priesthood lasted 40 years, serving 4 of those as a bishop and calling to mind the servant who reported back to his master, *'Master, you delivered to me five talents; here, I have made five talents more.'* (**Mt25:20**). These charisms are well illustrated in the rich testimonies provided by some priests and lay people in this book as well as the numerous condolence messages recorded which are only a snapshot of the outpouring grief witnessed by all who knew him when he passed away.

Bishop Munyongani was a gifted preacher, a teacher, a servant leader who loved and embedded himself within his people and above all, who was devoted to and served the Lord with his heart and soul. He touched the lives of multitudes of people both young and old during his time and this is ably narrated and illustrated in the text. His outstanding service in the priesthood culminated in his being sent by the Bishops' Conference to England in 2008 to serve the Zimbabwean Catholic community there as its inaugural Chaplain. We are aware too that his mission often extended beyond serving exclusively Catholic communities. *"You will receive power when the Holy Spirit comes on you; and you will be my witnesses in Jerusalem, and in all Judea and Samaria, and to the ends of the earth."* (**Acts1:8**)

In 2013 The Holy Father decided he was needed back home to continue service to the universal Church by appointing him bishop of Gweru diocese. In the Bishops' Conference we worked with Bishop Munyongani and we gratefully acknowledge the hard work, spirituality and wit that he wholeheartedly brought to our everyday work and for that we missed him dearly when God called him. We believe that he is now in a happier place full of joy and that he would have been found worthy of all the promises of Christ.

We pay due tribute to this humble priest from Mutero and hope this work by Mr Foroma of documenting works within the Church will be emulated by many others. We continue to pray that the Lord will grant us more vocations from men and women to serve in the vineyard where the harvest is plentiful but the labourers are few.

On behalf of the Zimbabwe Catholic Bishops' Conference (ZCBC)

✝ MICHAEL D BHASERA

Bishop of Masvingo

Table of Contents

	Foreword	7
1	**Introduction**	14
	1.1 The Mountain Has Fallen	19
2	**Catalogue of accomplishments**	23
	2.1 Xavier Munyongani, the early years	26
	2.2 The Pastoral Community	28
	2.3 The Diaspora Community	31
	2.4 The Charity Works	37
	2.5 The Social Being	39
	2.6 Small Christian Communities	42
	2.7 The Zimbabwe Catholic Men's Forum	45
	2.8 The Guild of St Joseph	48
	2.9 The Youth Ministry Within the Chaplaincy	49
	2.10 Some wounds we can see, others are hidden on the inside	51
3	**Working With Other Clergy**	55
4	**A Pastoral Visit with Fr Munyongani**	59
	4.1 A visit to the newly established Huntingdon Centre	59
	4.2 A Family Memorial Mass	61
	4.3 One of numerous practical homilies: Bishop Munyongani preaches development projects to his congregation 2017	63
	4.4 Fr Methuli Lanele Moyo on Sekuru Munyongani	66

| 5 | On Pilgrimage with Bishop Munyongani | 69 |
| 6 | Concluding Remarks | 72 |

Appendix 1:	The Testimonials	75
Appendix 2:	Recalling Some Condolence Messages: What the people said	116
Appendix 3:	Sekuru Munyongani's top drawer: What he used to say	122
Appendix 4:	Three Years On: celebrating the anniversary of his death: the grief lingers on	131
Appendix 5:	The story in pictures	139
Appendix 6:	Some special articles from Mr Benjamin Takavarasha's archival collections	150

ACKNOWLEDGEMENTS

My family supported my efforts to write and endured many hours without me while I persevered, often in solitude to compose and gather my thoughts to put pen to paper.

My close friends and brothers, Mr Christopher Mukopfa, Mr Harmless Pamburai and Mr Benjamin Takavarasha offered regular moral support, daily encouragement and a shoulder to lean on in difficult times so that I could go on to finalise this piece of work. Mr Takavarasha (Mukoma [*brother*] Benji as I call him) offered daily prayers, telling me always never to give up each time we spoke. Mrs Stella Kambarami joined me in a 14 day Novena to St Padre Pio to pray for the intercession of this great Saint for the successful completion of this work.

Mr Samuel Nhavira dutifully and painstakingly went through the whole draft to make numerous helpful and extremely constructive comments and suggestions.

This narrative was greatly enriched by the testimonies of 3 Catholic priests Fr Elias Chinzara, Fr Gilbert Tirivashoma Chibira and Fr Methuli Lanele Moyo and by 15 lay members of the Zimbabwe Catholic Community Chaplaincy in England and Wales. The lay members who shared their written testimonies which are reproduced in full in this publication are: Mr Samuel Nhavira, Mr Joseph Goredema, Mr Mavelos Madimu, Mrs Annie Kapungu, (young) Kumbirai Katema, Mr Benjamin Takavarasha, Mr Kizito and Mrs Cecelia Hakutangwi, Mrs Gertrude Mushayabasa, Mr Godfrey Mahaso, Dr Paul Matsvai, Mrs Albertina Bere, Mrs Connie Mutemachani, Mrs Eddah

Gatakata and Mr Claver Gozho. I owe these people an immeasurable debt of gratitude. Their contributions help to unpack who sekuru Munyongani the person was and offer reflections of their interactions and working with him in their own lives. I make special mention of the massive inspiration I drew from my friend Mrs Eddah Gatakata who even as she was already unwell, wrote her own testimony and actually frequently cajoled me to complete the rest of the manuscript! I am really grateful to Mr Ishevanhu Zengeya who very skilfully designed both the front and back covers of this book as a donation and has been a very supportive presence during the time I have worked on this book. Daniel Mutendi of DanTs Media Publishing also donated the layouts of the text and pictures and put up with the numerous changes that I requested always with a smile. I pray for all of these people each day for as Bishop Munyongani's favourite Psalm instructs us, *"What can I make to Yaweh for his generosity to me? I shall take up the cup of salvation and call on the name of Yaweh. I shall fulfil my vows to Yaweh, witnessed by all his people.."* **Ps116:12-14**

I have tried to take every care to present as accurate a narrative as possible but ultimately I take full responsibility for all inaccuracies and errors.

All net proceeds from this work are a donation to the Zimbabwe Catholic Bishops' Conference (ZCBC) as the life of the late bishop is a part of the Church and its preaching of the Good News of Jesus Christ.

1 Introduction

"Ndinoda kunangana nemi vana baba navana mai vemba!" (Meaning, 'I wish to focus on you men and women, the fathers and mothers of your households.' As an example, when I sit in that cubicle and ask you how long it is since you have been to the Sacrament of Confession you sheepishly say, "It has 'only' been six months, Father." Only 6 months! Nevertheless, I say go on, confess all your sins. And especially for the men, you say, 'It is only drunkenness, Father'. Really! You will perish in Hell with this type of behaviour. I also see smartly dressed grown men with beautiful pointed shoes nonchalantly making their way from the back of the Church, with no sense of shame or guilt about what they are about to do. I say where would you look if you tripped along the way and the 10 pence coin in your hand meant for the monthly Offertory spun away and hit one of these innocent Missionary Childhood little ones sat at the front or rolled and settled in front of the Choir over there? Would you pick it up and continue with your shameless act against The Lord? And as if that was not enough, when you leave the Church do you not go into the pub and offer lagers to however many of your friends happen to be around? I say, you must have a sense of perspective! Are the blessings you have not gifts from the Lord to whom you must express your deepest appreciation? Our God never goes to sleep, He sees every deed good and bad that you do, including seemingly minor actions such as offering drinking water to the thirsty. The choice is yours. Just like Joshua told the Israelites at Shekem!" *'Now therefore fear the Lord and serve him in sincerity and in faithfulness. Put away the gods that your fathers served beyond the River and in Egypt, and serve the Lord. And if it is evil in your eyes to serve the Lord, choose this day whom you will serve, whether the gods your fathers served in the region beyond the River, or the gods of the Amorites in whose land you dwell. But as for me and my house, we will serve the Lord.'* **Joshua24:14-15.**

"And to you the mothers. God gave us Mai Mariya (Our Lady the Blessed Virgin Mary) and other Saints like St Monica, St Anne, St Faustina, Mother Teresa of Calcutta, Elizabeth the mother of John the Baptist etc, the list goes on so we can have role models to follow.

"One day a husband returns from work earlier than usual and sadly says, 'Mother is no more. I came to tell you so we can pack and travel back to the village while it is still daylight.' Wife responds weakly, mumbling her expression of sadness at this tragedy and offering low key condolences. Slowly and leisurely she packs a few clothes for both of them and says they must pass by the vegetable market to load up a few cabbages for relish for the mourners as she could not afford to purchase beef or expensive provisions.

"And along the whole journey wife exudes a passive mood, soon nodding off. Later, branching off from the main motorway onto the rugged dusty road the wife jolts back awake and she remarks that it is now time to slip on her rough shoes for the rigours ahead. Husband and wife come from the same general locality in adjoining villages, and husband soon drives past the turn off to his own village homestead. Wife reminds him that he has just missed the turn to the village home. Husband apologetically says that he is aware but that he is going in the right direction. 'I said that mother has passed on.' It is then that wife realises that husband meant it was her mother who had died. I say to you mothers, you must not be so cruel. His parents and yours are all worthy of your respect in the eyes of the world and before God."

"I say to you all husbands and mothers, be very careful how you navigate your way in life, because you can cheat me, or all these people here but you cannot cheat God. He is all seeing and all knowing. And as for me, when we get to The Pearly Gates, I will say to God that you saw me preaching to these people in London, Northampton, Liverpool, Gokomere, Harare, Bulawayo, Rome, everywhere and anywhere. So, it is up to you Lord, I told them everything you sent me to teach them. So, you can sort them out yourself my Lord! ….and I will have nothing to do with you people as I will have told you everything God needs me to teach you."

Just one in tens of thousands of profound messages in his repertoire of homilies that Fr Munyongani regularly delivered to his faithful, suitably pitched so everyone could relate, understand and apply to their daily lives. Everyday. Every week. Every month. Every year. Those who had ears heard. But first things first. Let us go to the beginning.

At the time he was conferred the title of Monsignor, after being gently egged on to share some personal perspectives Fr Munyongani as he was then known, confided that his favourite passage from the Bible was Psalm 116 vs 11 - 17. And he liked the particular version from The New Jerusalem

Bible, and it had also been his late mother's favourite Psalm. He revealed that his mother had been the greatest influence on his joining the priesthood. Bless you Gogo (gran), and may you rest in eternal peace.

"In my terror I said, 'No human being can be relied on'. What can I make to Yaweh for his generosity to me? I shall take up the cup of salvation and call on the name of Yaweh. I shall fulfil my vows to Yaweh, witnessed by all his people. Costly in Yaweh's sight is the death of his faithful. I beg you Yaweh! I am your servant, and my mother was your servant; you have undone my fetters. I shall offer you a sacrifice of thanksgiving and call on the name of Yaweh." **Psalm 116 vs 11 – 17.**

"Pandakanga ndazunzika kudaro ndakati, 'Kuvimba nomunhu hakuna maturo.' Ko Tenzi ndichamupeiko pane zvizhinji zvaakandipa? Ndichapira mukombe woruponeso ndichindaidza zita raTenzi. Ndichaita zvandakatsidza kuna Tenzi vanhu vose vachiona. Kuna Tenzi, rufu rwavarurami vake rwakakosha. Tenzi ini ndiri muranda wenyu. Ndiri muranda wenyu, mwanakomana womurandakadzi wenyu, makandinunura kurufu. Ndichapira kwamuri chibayiro chokutenda ndichinamata zita raTenzi." **Psalm 116 vs 11 – 17.**

Years later……Bishop Munyongani at Regina Mundi Gweru, August 2017

"Ndongoitawo mafira kureva asi yavakusvika nguva yokuperavo kwangu. Ini ndakagadzwa musi wa 20 Aug

1977. Ndakagadzwa pamwe nababa Mutasa. Vakainda. Nababa David Mabhiza. Naivowo vakainda. Ndinosvitsa makore 40 ohupikiri neSvondo asi gare gare ndichaindavo, ndichida ndisingadi. Saka ndichakusiyai makadero kana musingadi kuchinja. Ndicho chokwadi chiri pachena ichi! Kana ndikasafa mumakore masere anotevera ndinenge ndozorega basa nokukura chero muchida musingadi. Asi ndakaedzawo. Ndakambozama. Makore mana ndiri muBishop, pamwe chete makumi mana ndiri mupriste. Chitendero changu ndakachiwana kunamai vakaita semi. Maita henyu. Mundinamatirewo........"

The final words of Bishop Munyongani at the end of the St Anne & St Joachim Feast Day celebration just before giving the final blessing during the Mass held at Regina Mundi, Gweru in August 2017.

"I will say this for what it is worth, the time is nearing when I may no longer be around. I was ordained a priest on 20 August 1977. I was ordained at the same time with Fr Mutasa. He is no more. And Fr David Mabhiza. He too is no more. On Sunday I will have been 40 years as a priest and sooner or later I will be gone whether I like it or not. But I will leave you as you are if you do not wish to change your ways. This is the naked truth. If I do not die earlier, in 8 years' time I will have to retire whether you like it or not. But I have tried my utmost. This coming Sunday I will have been a Bishop for 4 years of those 40 as a priest. My Catholic faith was handed down to me by a mother who was just like you. Thank you very much. Please pray for me."

Sekuru Munyongani's words before giving the final blessing at the end of Mass at Regina Mundi St Anne's Congress in 2017.

Was he perhaps foretelling his imminent departure?

1.1 The Mountain Has Fallen

To those of us in the diaspora Bishop Munyongani died twice: First on being recalled from the Chaplaincy community in England and Wales which he had served so well to take up the appointment as Bishop of Gweru diocese (even though we know it is part and parcel of the life of the Clergy and Religious to be rotated around the vineyard of The Lord for the greater good). And secondly, four years later, to eternity when the irreversible visited, the journey to the promised land. We mourned, even though we all knew we should have been celebrating his indomitable life. Within individuals and communities, the emotions were like random gigantic oceanic glaciers devoid of directional compasses amongst all those who had known him. On the one hand a deep and sad sense of deprivation that accompanies the realisation of a loss forever of that which we always casually took for granted and on the other, what should have been an acknowledgement of the greatness of a person who had become a part of everyone's household in the journeys of their joys and their miseries. The immediate aftermath of his passing was characterised by a period of paralysis, speechlessness and silent tears as thousands upon thousands of compassion messages were shared across the social media and at all community gatherings abroad and at home.

In 2017 Bishop Munyongani was diagnosed with cancer to which he succumbed on 15th October 2017 at the Avenues Clinic in Harare, aged only 67. After very emotional and well attended Vigils celebrating his gallant life held in Gweru and at Driefontein he was laid to rest at Driefontein Mission near Mvuma on Friday 20th October 2017. Masses were also celebrated for him across the country and abroad before and after his burial.

He was called from this earth----back to the Lord, perhaps holding in his hand the same promise Our Lady made to little St Bernadette Soubirous of Lourdes in 1858 to "**find happiness not in this but the other world.**" He had worked hard in this world. His reward would be elsewhere, in heaven. The message cannot be made forcefully enough that the passing of Bishop Munyongani should be a clarion call to the Church in Zimbabwe, that the time has come to start creating documented records of the local Church together with its icons, and Bishop Xavier is one of them. This is important for helping to perpetuate the Church of the future. The sad alternative being that if not captured, many invaluable lessons and memories from preachers, teachers, mentors, models of the highest calibre such as him simply dissipate with time into fading memories, eventually even nothingness. And yet there are many sons and daughters of Zimbabwe who continue to give their lives to God through the vocations or as the lay faithful to preach the Good News that need to be immortalised for posterity.

Even in death, he continued preaching the Good News as the coming together of diverse people and the testimonies given during his funeral was something seldom witnessed. Showing the whole world that one's good works will forever follow them. And completely unlike the political arena greatness of the spiritual type is not achieved as we have often seen, through the grabbing or legislating for power or descending to the levels of patronising communities in order to gain their "support". Or by haranguing, browbeating and forcefully harassing people into submission, so often characteristic of the landscape in both colonial and post-colonial Zimbabwe and elsewhere. He earned his dignity by living the truth and through prayer. Which enabled the power of The Holy Spirit to inspire him to lead the multitudinous flocks, holding the Holy Bible aloft simultaneously as his guiding compass and armour, and dutifully beaming the light and life of Christ to everyone all around. This was the Fr Xavier Munyongani we all came to know, love and respect. And the reason he continues to be missed with the gap he left being too huge to fill.

This humble and obedient servant from Mutero Mission, Gutu qualifies for special and honourable mention and should enter the annals of the Zimbabwean Catholic Church's recorded history. He belongs among the good and deserving, whom St Paul eloquently distinguishes in his Second Letter to Timothy as having *"…run the race, fought the good fight. And kept the faith"* **2Timothy4:7.**

Mhofu (Bishop Munyongani was affectionately called by his totem, Mhofu) ran his race well and fits the rich Shona description "Mbiru yeChitendero", a veteran of the faith in both flesh and heart, and most importantly, in spirit.

At his place of repose at Driefontein I was to find one of the largest piles of flowers adorning any one grave as I have ever seen. Signifying the simultaneous love and grief on the part of the community family in Zimbabwe and abroad who lovingly came to pay their respects and lay their beloved to rest. Many had been unable to make the actual funeral and continued to stream by to lay flowers and offer prayers at his shrine of repose.

As if planned Bishop Munyongani lies almost head to head in adjacent rows with the priest who was his first parish priest on leaving the Seminary in 1977, the late Fr Herman Nhariwa from Gokomere. Fr Nhariwa was the parish priest at St Anthony's Mission in Zaka when the young Fr Munyongani was posted there on leaving Chishawasha Seminary. As you would expect from two bubbly personalities, they immediately struck up a wonderful working relationship in both their personal and spiritual work. Fr Nhariwa died only a few months later in December 1977 a mere half a year after the two started working together at St Anthony's. Fr Munyongani often reflected on many fond memories of "Sarirambi", this energetic priest and their time together in Zaka, a fellow "Mhofu" like himself. He was a priest who seemed to occupy a special place in Fr Munyongani's heart. We pray that these two priests who worked together and were fortuitously reunited in their final earthly resting places have also both been glorified in the Kingdom of heaven.

Many people will have memories and reflections about the late Bishop Munyongani. Many such stories will resonate with the recorded observations here but some may not, and can be different, and so they should. More people should take to writing about our Catholic faith. The history of the Church in Zimbabwe is hardly documented. This narrative is a small contribution towards that effort.

2 Catalogue of accomplishments

I was privileged during his Chaplaincy years to work with Fr Munyongani, later Monsignor and even later as Bishop elect. We shared a happy, friendly and enduring working relationship. The decision to write these reflections partly stems from that. It is also out of a sense of duty to record something about our faith. Much appreciation is due to the wide cross section of parishioners who worked with or knew the late Bishop in various capacities who kindly agreed to share their own reflections and testimonies as part of this collection.

First in his formative life it was the call to the priesthood. Like Samuel in the Bible, he responded with humility "*Speak my Lord your servant is listening.*" 1 Samuel 3:9. And then after 40 years in that vineyard of the Lord, God called again. This time he was being called home. He responded to both (how could he not?). Obediently, having accomplished and distinguished himself as a true servant in the vineyard. With outstanding, resounding and impeccable service to God and

His people, reverberating all corners of the globe, his job here on earth was done.

All done through the Holy Spirit, some real-life examples being:
- The work he carried out among the Catholic faithful in Zimbabwe and then as Chaplain to the Zimbabwean Catholic Community in England and Wales;
- The converts he brought to the Church;
- The souls he brought back from the brink;
- Those lapsed faithful he so ably and tactfully coaxed, winning them back to the faith and into the fold;
- Those who had given up all hope on account of the vicissitudes of this earthly life;
- The institutions of the Church he served and those he built. The parishes he presided over;
- The hundreds of priests he trained: both as Church history lecturer and Vice Rector of Chishawasha Regional Major Seminary;
- The new ground he often broke spreading The Good News. Yes, those firebrand homilies!
- On numerous occasions ministering to the sick some of whom knew him but had never dreamt it might be him to give those rites;
- Ministering to those who never knew him but who found him at their doorstep and bedside at their hour of greatest need;
- Those who fell silent and went to sleep and had known him but did not in their lives think it might be him coming to take them on the journeys to their final resting places;
- The many baptisms;
- The First Holy Communions;
- The Confirmations;

- The Weddings;
- The journeys into the vocations he not only influenced but presided over;
- The marriages and relationships he frequently salvaged from cliff hanger situations at home and in the diaspora through prayerful, persistent and tactful shepherding, particularly during his time in the diaspora;
- The persistent reminders to the faithful to not forget their Zimbabwean values through a misinterpretation or misconception of their newfound "freedoms" or "rights" in an alien land;
- The courtships he mentored spiritually until the "till death do us part…" vows were eventually made in front of contented families and appreciating communities.

In 2016 and 2017 there were no less than 6 weddings among the Catholic youths in the England and Wales Zimbabwean community (I teasingly refer to these youngsters as '*the class of '92*' after one of the most successful Manchester United academy cohort of young footballers progressed to its first team in the early 1990s). Fr Munyongani mentored this group of youths, which to this day remains the biggest and most active and well networked group of young couples in the history of the Zimbabwean Catholic Chaplaincy in this country. Of course, these young people received the help and support from their own families and friends as does everyone else, but this success happened under the late Bishop's watch as Chaplain and more, much, much more. Perhaps his enduring legacy will one day repeat itself, as history always does, when a future Chaplaincy will one day be presided over by a beautiful blend of Clergy and laity whose green shoots will be traceable to its own Chaplaincy days or significant future works of God. Some may say but this is what is expected and indeed routinely discharged by every priest. The difference is the extent and zeal with which each accomplishment was achieved. He always executed each task with the utmost passion and exacting dedication to duty, one might perhaps even say, beyond normal call of duty. For ever stretching himself even when his advancing years, combined with health challenges visibly exacted their toll and strain on his routines. His gaze undoubtedly permanently fixated on Christ and His Mother Mai Mariya: Fr Xavier Munyongani the ultimate humble priest.

2.1 Xavier Munyongani, the early years

Bishop Xaverio Johnsai Munyongani was born on 1 January 1950 at Mutero Mission in Gutu district in the Diocese of Masvingo. His parents Joachim and Anna were blessed with 10 children, of whom Xaverio, more commonly known as Xavier was the eighth child. In his priestly days he was affectionately called "Mhofu", his totem (also Museyamwa, Shava, Mwendamberi etc). This totem is the animal generally known as the Eland. In Zimbabwean African culture every person has an animal, bird or object (totem) by which members of their clan lineage is known and is often used in preference to using the actual name as a mark of respect, love, affection, dignity and identity for the particular individual.

After his primary education at schools in Gutu district, he completed his secondary education at the Gweru diocesan

Minor Seminary of Chikwingwizha (1967-1970). Later he joined Chishawasha Regional Major Seminary just outside Harare for his Philosophy and Theology studies (1971-1977).

He was ordained a priest for the diocese of Gweru, on 20 August 1977 by the then (late) Bishop of Gweru, Rt Rev Tobias Chiginya.

In 2007, the Zimbabwe Catholic Bishops' Conference (ZCBC) appointed him the inaugural formal Chaplain of the Zimbabwean Catholics in England and Wales, a post he took up on 18 June 2008. In recognition of his continuing exemplary priestly life and meritorious pastoral zeal for the Church in Zimbabwe, Pope Benedict XVI elevated and conferred upon Fr Xavier Munyongani the title of "Monsignor in The Papal Household" in 2010.

He was appointed Bishop of Gweru on 15th June 2013 and ordained as the Bishop of that diocese on 14th September that same year.

As our Chaplain, with his booming voice and infectious personality, the life of Bishop Munyongani was a larger than life phenomenon even before his sad and untimely passing. His cheerful persona, charism, wit, intellect, profound knowledge and dedication to the Catholic Faith always gave you the unspoken shivers that there were many special things about this person that would one day be missed, most likely with everyone being caught off guard when it happened. And judging by the outpouring of grief, emotion and effortless tears when he passed away, this was a day many preferred should never have seen the light of day, so to speak.

When Bishop Munyongani died on Sunday 15th October 2017, the Catholic communities in the diaspora and in Zimbabwe fell silent in unison to mourn the death of a gallant son of the soil and true servant of the Lord. A friend of the people. Everyone's friend, young and old, mentor, teacher, counsellor, preacher, advisor, defender of the rights of others, a thinker, a leader, a mediator. The list goes on. Perhaps most of all, PREACHER, an example to all of us. With knowing precision, he would pinpoint the exact source of almost any passage or event from The Holy Bible. If you were seeking advice or counsel, you always got an immediate response and it would dawn on you then that he had heard and seen it all before. Fount of knowledge and advice. Such was his prowess in the work he loved and lived for. Bishop Munyongani touched the lives and livelihoods of people beyond the Catholic Church too. As Chaplain to the Catholic Community in England and Wales he often he led his Catholic faithful in large numbers to periodic multi denominational Christian gatherings in the UK where he earned the respect of the pastors and followers of other denominations. At that forum he was unanimously deferred to as the best placed person to become the spiritual advisor of the multi denominational Zimbabwean Christian Men's Fellowship (ZCMF) which also included the Catholic men. All these and many other non-Catholics who knew him felt the same deep sense of loss as us when news broke that he was no more.

2.2 The Pastoral Community

During the Chaplaincy years Fr Munyongani, later Monsignor and then Bishop-elect interacted with everyone in the community. Young, old, black, white, Catholic, non-Catholic, anyone. He was multilingual too being fluent in Shona, Ndebele, Italian and German. And with most people if he asked and you told him or described where you came from in Zimbabwe, he either had been there or had some local knowledge of the place. Or knew some people in those parts, or even something witty about the place! The master of wit and joke with his perpetually happy and positive demeanour. Around him you just loosened up and liked this priest. There were many occasions and moments we shared, joyful, reflective. Sometimes difficult and sad as when there was bereavement or sickness in the community, and at other times difficult choices or pragmatic management decisions. It was all such an honour to work for and with him, all the time learning and absorbing what he demonstrated through his humble and hugely infectious personality. But most of all to see how he was working so reverently and determinedly for his Lord through the people gathered before him. Perhaps the best way to remember Bishop Munyongani would be to continue the work he was doing and what he stood for. And to learn the many lessons from his work so we can use them as signposts in our own lives. In the rich Shona language articulately fashioned by our elders, conversation is frequently punctuated by folk sayings and proverbs. One such is *"Ivhu ndiro rinoziva kuti mwana wembeva anorwara"* (It is the soil that understands and knows that a baby mouse is unwell). This saying captures the late Bishop's art of community leadership. I learnt from the late Bishop that if you wish to lead people successfully you have to become one of them. An integral part of them. And as you lead, you must constantly put yourself in their shoes, frequently asking yourself, "What would I do in their situation?" You have to fully relate to all their situations, being with them when they grieve, celebrating their joys and their successes with them. A leader must be in the present with the people they lead. The late Zimbabwean politician Maurice Nyagumbo in his autobiography, "**With the People**" put it well when he gave insights into his own nationalism. He passionately lamented...."*some of us must remain behind to be with the people....even if often it means to be in jail with them*". Nyagumbo's reflections explain why African nationalism was able to triumph over colonialist settler rule in Rhodesia. A failure to understand this important principle is in my view why many politicians, including some Church leaders are major culprits in the failures and lack of progress of their communities after what are usually promising early years. Economics Professor Raja Chelliah from the Indian Institute of Public Finance and Policy once told me, "*If you want the best out of people, release the energies of those people.*" To be successful a manager has to enable each individual to perform in the area they excel the most and to the best of their abilities, and allowing people to "own" the successes they achieve, rather than shackling people's efforts and initiatives with controls or in some cases even appearing to be competing with them. Our Church leaders and politicians could learn here from the late Munyongani.

Like everyone Fr Munyongani will have had faults of his own as a mortal being. But he clearly understood what it meant to stand with and be with the people. This important attribute of his is frequently lost when people focus more on the practical jokes, the humour and wit that characterised his preaching of The Good News and his personality without focussing on the deeper messages. And some focussed on the fact that he seemed to be related to everyone in the community when really it was being with the people being put in action!

2.3 The Diaspora Community

The Zimbabwe Catholic community in England and Wales is dispersed all over England from North to South, and East to West. The community is structured into 'Centres' that are timetabled to regularly congregate at more than a dozen Centres with each Centre getting a weekend Chaplaincy Mass once a month. A Centre is a geographical location (usually a town) where the number of faithful have been able to organise (or the potential exists to so organise) themselves into a critical number of the faithful to have Mass celebrated for them and for the faithful to mobilise themselves into at least one Small Christian Community. A Centre may have a size considered reasonable to have a separate community Mass given the distances to the next Centre where Zim Catholics gather under the auspices of the Chaplaincy. The establishment of the Centres took into account the numbers of existing priest(s) being able to include such Centre in the timetable for one Mass visit within a calendar month (some smaller Centres in the earlier years used to have Masses less frequently than monthly).

Notwithstanding the establishment of these Centres, the faithful were regularly reminded and expected by the Chaplain to attend the weekly Masses in their own local parishes (and many now have roles in their local parishes as parish committee members, Mass servers, Eucharistic Ministers of the Holy Communion, Readers, Ushers etc). Thus, the establishment of the Zimbabwean Chaplaincy was never meant to replace or be in competition with the role of the local parishes, but rather to complement each other in a special way thereby enhancing the faith of the Catholic faithful. This model of Centres has been adopted as a template for the development of the Catholic faith in other parts of the world where Zimbabwean Catholics reside.

London is the principal and main Centre and the Chaplaincy is accredited to England and Wales through the Catholic Archdiocese of Westminster in London. Through the good offices of the Archdiocese of Westminster the Chaplain and his assistant are also accommodated at two parishes in North London (though one has now moved to the North West). The London community (to which I belong) meets at Stoke Newington for the monthly Mass on the first Saturday of each month. London is loosely defined here as the faithful from as far as Southampton, Portsmouth, Essex, and the other home counties to form a large congregation of up to 250 at each monthly Mass. Other centres spread around the country are found in places such as Luton, Coventry, Birmingham, Leicester, Leeds, Sheffield, Manchester, Liverpool, Bolton, Huntingdon, Bedford, Milton Keynes. Numbers of the faithful at each centre vary because of the differing sizes of the catchment areas, or the ability of the local nucleus community to mobilise their people to come forward. In many respects the diaspora community reflects the Zimbabwean community from which it derives.

Our people left the mother country Zimbabwe in search of better opportunities and relief from the economic, social and political meltdown in the county for themselves and their children. They very admirably carried with them their Catholicity into exile and maintained it and this has been a very positive and shining aspect of the Zimbabwean Catholics. Zimbabweans have carried this not just to England and Wales but to other parts of the globe too where Zimbabweans have gone and championed their faith. People of other faiths too carried their Christian denominations into the diaspora. So, while the Catholic community is the largest and perhaps most organised faith in the UK diaspora, we have come to know and relate to numerous colleagues from Zimbabwe who belong to other faith denominations as well.

Within the community itself there were some dynamics at play. For some the economic and social pressures in their new diaspora environment and the "fish-out-of-water" experiences of a community displaced and thrown into an alien setting with little or no preparation exerted a heavy and costly toll. Many had simply wanted to be able to earn an honest dollar (or Pound) to feed their families. Yet in some families however both spouses did not always agree or manage to or even want to come to the UK. So, some families lived split lives, some broke up in the process. Some young people were brought up in families where either or both parents had fallen prey to the "fish-out-of-water" experience as some lost their values and self-worth.

Many Zimbabweans in the diaspora had left behind what had been senior and well-paying jobs at home to re-start their lives in the UK carrying out menial jobs, a sea change from their training and previous comfort zones. The economic meltdown and lack of hope at home literally drove millions of citizens outside the borders of their own country in search of a new life. The consequential desperation and obligatory retraining meant some of the people having to endure the humiliation and frustration in midlife as they restarted their careers at the bottom of the ladder in the new workplace. These frustrations caused depression, anger, and sometimes despair among our people. The UK employment market did not always offer our people meaningful opportunities to make progress beyond the entry levels to most jobs. The majority had to train or retrain in the healthcare professions, social work or took positions as industrial shop floor operatives. Though mostly hard working to exemplary levels Zimbabweans encountered issues in the workplaces where they had to acclimatise to a new work environment with different work ethics to what they were used to.

Within families there were often role reversals with many women folk entering the nursing and health care professions which offered easier visa and resident permits than some of their male counterparts. Sometimes, for the first time both husband and wife ended up in the same jobs as nurses or care workers or warehouse operatives. All these and many other social and economic pressures played havoc on the domestic relationships within families. Some mistakenly felt "liberated" to experience a life where the social norms and mores were no longer governed by the traditional guidelines and expectations of Zimbabwean extended family society due to working in locations where they were cut off from anyone they knew or could "see" in their daily lives. Some strayed into lives that would not be tolerated or looked at favourably back home or by their kith and kin. Of course, there were many more who kept their heads and survived these blowing winds in the diaspora.

Such was the mixed and varied environment and the challenges that Fr Munyongani came to operate in. A community and individuals generally being suffocated by newtonian pressures from all directions: in their own mother country which they had run away from, in the new setting where they now lived and the third dimension being their direct or extended family whom they had left behind who saw those who had gone abroad as their lifeline to get support to procure food, cash for educating the young ones and other essentials to support life, all with no obvious signs of respite within sight. Some slowly drifted away from the Catholicism under which they were brought up. But luckily many kept their faith and made possible the symbiotic relationship they had with their Chaplain, making the ZimChaplaincy such a model of the success of faith in a diaspora context that has not been seen in too many places. The community has much to be applauded for making the whole Chaplaincy mission such a success. Many

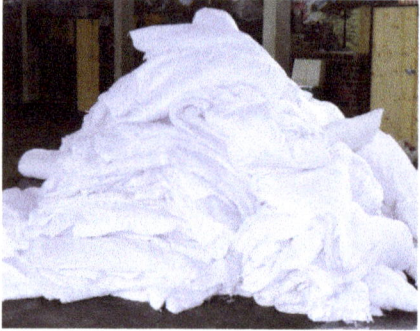

A variety of charitable goods which included school books, appliances, linens, clothing for orphanages, items for the elderly Clergy and Religious etc. In the top two photos items are being packed pre-shipping, and bottom photos shipment has been unloaded in Zimbabwe and being prepared for distribution to the needy. This is only a small insight into the numerous charitable works he shepherded with the England and Wales Catholic faithful.

denominations often quoted the vibrancy of the Catholic community as a model to emulate.

Fr Munyongani presided over the consolidation of the Community's dozen Centres around the country, strengthening Guild activities and other Liturgical aspects of the faith in the process. And a rapidly growing and vibrant Youth component in the Community will be another lasting legacy. On weekly Chaplaincy Centre visits, Fr Munyongani often stayed with families in the areas he would celebrate Mass: a priest deeply embedded in the lives of the people he was serving.

2.4 The Charity Works

Many Catholics have invested huge efforts to maintain active contact with the Church back home and to grow their children in Catholicism. It was the harnessing of this zeal to pray and maintain their faith that Fr Munyongani was asked to come to England and Wales to ignite, fan, and grow this faith as Chaplain to the Zimbabwean Catholics. As key pillars of his work with the community, many charitable resources were mobilised over the years to support communities and institutions back home. Fr Munyongani and other priests were at the heart of these efforts, often seen manually loading container loads of donations to be shipped. Sometimes returning from a pastoral visit or a Centre Mass Fr Munyongani would on some occasions be seen bringing back a bag or two of clothes and toiletries given by a well-wisher family so these could be loaded and shipped to the needy in Zimbabwe.

He breathed and lived charity. His frequent refrain, "*Faith without works is dead.*" *(Chitendero chisina mabasa chakafa)* **James 2:26** became a common refrain among the faithful too. Charitable works supporting good causes such as the Seminarians in Zimbabwe, retirement houses for the Clergy and Religious, old people's homes and orphanages became signature activities of this Chaplain. The whole community took to this work and each year a container load of charitable items was shipped to Zimbabwe. This project which started as an annually shipped 20 ft container expanded into a 40 ft container annually by the time he left to return to Zimbabwe to become Bishop of Gweru. It had also grown from one which the London based Catholic faithful spearheaded to one in which the whole Chaplaincy took ownership even though the financing and logistics remained the sole responsibility of the London Centre. It was a truly unifying project among the faithful as people could engage in charitable works across the different Chaplaincy centres and geography, while providing much needed help to the communities in the motherland. One Pentecostal church leader once remarked, "You Catholics are doing such a marvellous job and even though we may not say so, we are learning so much and admiring the wonderful work you are doing."

The community's warmth and identification with Fr Munyongani's charitable outlook was clearly noticeable in its generosity and enthusiasm towards works of mercy. A shepherd and a community who achieved a perfect meeting of the minds, locking horns around good causes whilst relentlessly executing any project embarked upon. A perfect blend. Again here we see Fr Munyongani's management style getting the most out of people.

Fr Munyongani's Homilies at Centre Masses, whole community Chaplaincy Masses, always reminded the faithful to underpin their faith with works of mercy. Over the years I witnessed a number of people who either returned to the Catholic faith or converted to Catholicism because of their encounters with Fr Munyongani. Ordinary folks witnessed his down to earth ways and the carrying out works of faith breaking sweat, a display of grey dishevelled hair and the undone shirt of a man at work. These things touched the hearts and preached the Good News more than any words could express.

2.5 The Social Being

There were lighter moments too. Often at the end of a long day after the monthly Mass in London a few of us would at his invitation, just sit around and share conversation, light-hearted chit chat about this and that. Also an informal feedback session about how the day would have gone. On some Saturday evenings his favourite football team Barcelona FC would be playing in the Spanish League, La Liga. "*Simbi inogaya dzimwe*!" (Metal making short work of other metals) as he called his team when Barcelona inevitably scored and thrashed other teams as they always did. We shared his joys with him. These seemed clearly to be some of his happiest moments of light relief egging his team on. Sitting with him to share the magic of his team applying their 'tiki-taka' football to demolish their lesser Spanish opponents, or other European clubs was always special for him. In between he would keep you entertained with jokes and anecdotes. All of this was light-hearted, harmless humour. He was human after all. Every one of us needs renewal. His emphasis and devotion to prayerfulness at Centre and Small Christian Community (Section) Masses was a permanent mark that he left in the Community, and the singing too.

In all his work he would not admit that he was tired, as long as there was shepherding work to be done. He would say that we would all rest on the day the Lord calls us and that we must all just work for now. One day in July 2011 having spent the night at a Guild All-night event out of town, he came back to the London Centre Mass and on this occasion, fatigue took its toll. It was left to other co-celebrating priests to lead the Mass as he was unable to continue a few minutes after the Mass had started and had to go and have a rest. An abiding affinity to duty. Part of his persona. But even he too tires, he was human after all like the rest of us.

I often wondered, till I got to know him a little better, why nearly everyone in the community was either Mukuwasha, Vatezvara, Sekuru, Muzukuru, munin'ina, Hanzvadzi, Tete (son in law, brother in law, father in law, uncle, grandfather, grandmother, nephew, niece, sister, auntie etc). I have known in traditional African culture that many people in the community will in one way or another always be your relatives, but Fr Munyongani took this to a whole new level... The words in John18 vs 9 "Not one of those you gave me have I lost" come to mind, he wanted everyone to feel wanted and belong, to make everyone feel special and valued.

Even after he had become Monsignor if you happened to miss a telephone call from him and he left a message for you, it was always, "It is me Fr Munyongani who had called...." He never used the title Monsignor on himself. Nor did he go about reminding everyone he was the Chaplain. Ultimate humility. If he was speaking to someone on the phone the respect and dignity, he gave the other person would make you think he was speaking to his own mother or parent, a lesson for all of us.

If you spent any time with him you were always struck by the incessant ringing of his phone, from very early in the morning to well after the normal social hours at night. Parishioners and others from all corners of the Chaplaincy calling him to liaise or arrange community activities or seeking help or spiritual and moral support. Or in tears to report the death or illness of a loved one either in the UK or back home.

In the eyes of his superiors at the Archdiocese of Westminster in London he did much to enhance the profile and perception of the Zimbabwean Chaplaincy as a model Chaplaincy amongst those that are based in the UK. The then Auxiliary Bishop in charge of Ethnic Chaplaincies always held out the Zimbabwean Chaplaincy as a model Chaplaincy that was well behaved and well managed. Of course, there was a lot of ground work already previously done by another priest, Fr Athanasio Dzadagu who had initiated the work of getting Zimbabweans to get together to pray well before the formal Chaplaincy was established. A similar picture was also reflected within the realm of the African Chaplaincies where the Zimbabwean Chaplaincy enjoyed an unblemished record and often relied on to participate in Liturgical activities at such events as the Annual African Chaplaincies Mass, or the annual Dowry of Mary Pilgrimage to The Shrine of Our Lady of Walsingham in East Anglia. Because the Catholic Church in England is in many ways different to the Zimbabwean Catholic way of Liturgy Fr Munyongani explained to the Archdiocese of Westminster WHY his community needed to do certain things the "Zimbabwean way" and he was always allowed to shepherd his flock in ways they were familiar with according to their Zimbabwean roots.

Even to this day on pilgrimages to Walsingham days the local Bishop who used to be Auxiliary Bishop at Westminster always looks out to see the members of the Zimbabwean Chaplaincy and asks if we have come with priests from the Chaplaincy. Such still is the legacy of the late Bishop Munyongani on the senior hierarchy of the Catholic Church in the UK.

2.6 Small Christian Communities

Small Christian communities were some of the favourite groups of the faithful Fr Munyongani encouraged and regularly interacted with. He would say, "*I go on Centre pastoral visits away from London at weekends. This generally means I travel out of London on Friday afternoons or Saturday or Sunday mornings. During the rest of the time, I am available here to assist the host parish with Masses and other work, but I am available to meet with your Sections and to celebrate Masses in your localities. Use me!*" As a result of these exhortations and ready availability of our Chaplain, the Small Christian communities around London really took off and had frequent evening house Masses, or weekday evening Masses celebrated in local parishes, very often concelebrated with the local parish priest if he was available. These Masses whenever possible would be preceded by Confessions, and sometimes ended with the Exposition of The Blessed Sacrament. Many of us were drawn to review our Catholic practices and to recognise that we had not nearly been doing enough or as much as we could as we had disguised ourselves behind the thin alibi of 'busy and irregular shift work patterns'. Sometimes two neighbouring Christian communities joined together to celebrate Mass with the Chaplain and this helped to provide mutual support and to get parishioners to bond with each other at the local levels. A while ago I was chatting with a friend who has now risen to become an active and prominent lay leader in the Chaplaincy. He confessed thus,

"You know when Fr Munyongani came to this section and celebrated Mass at the house not far from my own for a lady who was sick, I came to realise that through her own confession that although that lady was Catholic, she had not been coming to Church at all and not making any contributions to support the Chaplaincy. I and the whole of my family were not coming to Church either and were not even going to the local parish even

though we were also Catholic. That became the day my whole outlook of the Church and the Chaplaincy changed, and I started to encourage my family to go to Church. We have not looked back ever since."

We used to joke that when Fr Munyongani came to the Section Mass, he would conduct "pre-preaching preaching"! Because that is how seriously he took his ministry. He would explain the Readings that would be used during Mass and we would even sing some songs as preparation before Mass started. He would ask the person taking the first Reading to stay on until after he himself had read the Gospel and afford that Reader a few minutes to say what had caught their heart in both the first Reading and the Gospel. This was massively helpful training in preaching skills to the laity which would help us to pray and preach at community prayer sessions and bereavements when no priest was available. We began to grow in the faith and to have the confidence to take responsibility to pray for others.

Bereavement is one of the most inconvenient occurrences in our humanly lives but it is inevitable. Whilst in the lay leadership, at any time of day a phone call or a social media message would come through announcing the passing on of someone in our community, or someone known by a member of the community, or a family member back home. The oneness inculcated in us by the Chaplain in such situations compelled us to spread the word around quickly and inform the Chaplain who himself would drop everything at once and ask us to set in motion arrangements for the celebration of Mass that very evening or the next possible day after. He would often visit the sick on his own during the week when he understood most of his lay leaders would be at work.

2.7 The Zimbabwe Catholic Men's Forum

Serving as a London Centre committee member one day I asked Fr Athanasio Dzadagu if we could do something to ensure there was more participation by the men in the Church. Fr Dzadagu was the priest who initiated and had been looking after the Zim Catholic community before its formalisation as a Chaplaincy. His polite and diplomatic response to my question was that this was an issue he was aware of, and which had been tried in the past but without much success. When I offered to make another effort, he was magnanimous enough to agree and immediately offered any help he could as it was an issue very close to his own heart. After exploring several options, the preferred one was not to have a specific Guild but to have a 'forum' to which all men would be welcome. Fr Munyongani took his position as Chaplain at this point. It is to his great credit as a leader that he did not arrive and proceed to disband this work in progress. Instead he instantly recognised this as one of the key pillars of the work he needed to do and immediately put shoulder to wheel and helped refine the forum proposals. Fr Munyongani suggested what turned out to be a gem of strategy to get the idea to succeed: canvassing the womenfolk to get their husbands and mature sons to come to Leicester on 19th July for the grand launch of the men's group.

A total of 75 Catholic men from all over the newly recognised Chaplaincy gathered for the meeting.

Fr Munyongani frequently described this Forum, aimed at getting the Catholic men across the whole Chaplaincy to be more prayerful and worthy Christian leaders of their households while participating more visibly in the Church as, *"Dhamu rakazara nehove dzemhando dzose, matatya, makakanje nezvimwe zvipuka asi matinoda kunyurura hove chete"*. (A dam full of fish of all types fish, frogs, crabs and other unseemly creatures, but from which we wish to extract fish only.) In a logical, measured and tactful trajectory.

Later at one of our meetings of the Men's Forum it was agreed that the men each make a contribution in order to buy the Chaplain a vehicle for use in his pastoral work. The decision was promptly and unanimously adopted by all present and the various chapters of the Forum at each of the Chaplaincy's centres offered to coordinate the collection of funds among their local members. This plan worked so well that within the month, enough funds had been put together to buy the priest's car. A small team was then tasked to do the actual procurement of the vehicle to use in his pastoral ministry. So it was that Fr Munyongani was handed his car to use as Chaplain to the community. The novice group of men was at last beginning to show its mettle and taking its place as leaders of the community which had hitherto predominantly been spearheaded by the women. The other Guilds stepped in to show their support by offering to help with items such as insurance, road tax, essential repairs as and when they happened etc. Faith with works as preached by St James was clearly at play here.

On another occasion after Fr Munyongani was elevated to the title of Monsignor, the Men's Forum pooled together again and purchased a head to toe set of vestments for his new role as Monsignor. And then exceptionally, one member of the forum quietly made arrangements to singlehandedly provide an additional set of vestments as had been provided by the other men for which he had also made his contribution, making light of his contribution by saying he simply wanted the Chaplain to have a change of vestments when one set was being laundered! Another wonderful example of the faith amongst the men. "When Jesus heard this, he was amazed at him, and turning to the crowd following him, he said, *"I tell you, I have not found such great faith even in Israe*l." Luke 7:9. There is an intrinsic desire to do good in all of us and while some are more able to show this spontaneously, as this man and his family did, some need a trigger or to be prompted in the direction of acting positively and this is where the role of community lay leadership plays an invaluable role.

At Masses and community gatherings Fr Munyongani would always joke that the community should desist from ruffling his "Form 4's" (meaning the Men's Forum members), whom he considered a fragile work in progress needing to be mentored with care and sensitivity until its maturity. This comment always had congregations almost falling off their pews in stitches, but actually had a much deeper and serious meaning beyond the light-hearted apprenticeship references it was accorded. He sensed that having been able to prise away many men of all manner of activities which had kept them away from the Church he did not want this precious work to be "damaged" by casual or insensitive treatment before they were fully tried and tested.

2.8 The Guild of St Joseph

From this group of men in the forum the Chaplaincy was able to reap some very handsome results. From them it was possible to mobilise the continuation and establishment of the St Joseph's Guild in England and Wales in its current form. Many men joined the St Joseph's Guild. As Fr Munyongani had correctly predicted, the men's forum became the maternity ward from which the Guild of St Joseph was re-birthed in the diaspora. Other men joined other Guilds such as the Sacred Heart of Jesus or the St Joachim's Guild. The forum has been a source from which much spirituality poured forth. There are many men too who preferred not to join any of the Guilds but who nevertheless have now stepped forward to serve the Church as tireless foot soldiers in numerous admirable ways. The point was always made to the faithful that it was alright for anyone who did not feel inclined to belong to a Guild to remain so as the primary call was for everyone to become members of the Church of Christ. Guild membership was only an additional desirable but not obligatory devotion to aid people's journeying towards the promised land in heaven.

The seed Fr Munyongani and his fellow priests were on mission to establish was bearing fruit. *"I have come to bring fire on the earth, and how I wish it were already kindled!"* **Luke12:49**.

2.9 The Youth Ministry Within the Chaplaincy

Reference has already been made to the huge successes with the Youth ministry which resulted in lifelong networks and partnerships amongst the youth of the Chaplaincy which has not been replicated after his departure. The secret seems to have been a combination of his charisms of embedding himself in the work of any section of the community, combined with fully delegating to the laity the roles of 'uncles' and 'aunties' of the youth so they felt fully empowered to carry out their work of evangelising to the Youth with accountability for their actions. Successes in the ministries were always attributed to the communities themselves and this always engendered ownership and following from this a spirit of always wanting to achieve even more than before, a form of community participation in the affairs of the parishioners by the community itself.

Another aspect was the involvement of the younger priests sent to the UK by their Bishops for post graduate studies. Always welcoming each of them warmly on their on arrival in England and with all of them having been his former students the stage was set very early on for these priests to work with the Chaplain and his community. With the priests themselves being much younger, they could readily relate to the younger people in the community and understand their 'language', Fr Xavier himself always being available to give support and liven things up for the youth programmes. Programmes to deliberately provide opportunities and support for the youth were prioritised within the Chaplaincy: funds were generously made available to promote youth activities and with the youth themselves being involved in projects meant for their welfare. With several young priests available as mentor and spiritual directors for youth activities, the framework was set for the youth ministry to flourish. The icing on the cake was the encouragement for the youth to be involved in the main Liturgical activities periodically leading community Masses and holding their own annual congresses, opportunities to fundraise locally at various Centre Masses and having their own regular meetings before the monthly Chaplaincy Masses. There was a lot more method and management philosophy to the outgoing personality exuded by the Chaplain.

It was not surprising that in 2011 when the World Youth Day (WYD) which was held in Madrid about 30 young people from the Chaplaincy participated. The WYD is a worldwide encounter between the youth from around the world and The Holy Father celebrated about every three years in a different country. Since then there has been not been another global stage participation by our youth larger than this one. My daughter Agatha Kuziva, then a youth herself and a part of this group reflected:

"Despite the slightly disappointing start with our group flying out on a rearranged flight after missing our scheduled flight Fr Munyongani led us into our pilgrimage in Madrid. The accommodation and facilities were not great, but it was so special to be amongst other young people from across the globe in a wonderfully spiritual environment. You may not speak the same language, but you still have the mutual understanding of why you are all in the same venue. To have the programme and Mass celebrated by The Holy Father with our own Fr Munyongani in that unending procession of hundreds of priests from all over the world was surreal. It was really cool. Unforgettable. I will live with that experience forever."

2.10 Some wounds we can see, others are hidden on the inside

The subject of the loss of a loved one is a most difficult part of everyone's life. In Zimbabwean culture death has always been a taboo subject and one that understandably brings sadness, grief and difficult emotions to anyone. Some points however need to be referenced regarding the uniqueness of life in the diaspora. Many years before even the Chaplaincy was established I got to know of a tragic case where a Zimbabwean lady passed away unnoticed in her single room accommodation. Her routine was allegedly one of working, and working, and working and then just keeping to herself on her off days without really engaging with neighbours or having a meaningful social life that anyone was aware of. It came to pass that the first her neighbours knew something was amiss was when they began to experience an increasingly uncomfortable waft from her room when passing by the vicinity of her lodgings. And it was left to the police to confirm the grim death from unknown causes and then trying to use sparse information to determine her identity and next of kin. In the end Zimbabwean London embassy staff had to collect her modest belongings and ship these to her next of kin back home.

The establishment of the Chaplaincy community solved some of the problems of isolation and loneliness by creating a rallying point as people began to worship together, grow their social networks and comradeships amongst themselves.

But there was another dimension that was hardly scratched perhaps even skin deep. It is the issue of dealing with grief and the situation unfortunately remains so to this day. Back in Zimbabwe communities are structured geographically in close proximity and the large number of the extended families around provide much needed support and care when needed. In the diaspora life is a relentless 24/7 cycle in which people are required to fit into this permanent round robin. The economies in which people live are designed such that people work to earn cash which seems programmed to be poured back into the 'system' in the form of taxes, bills, utilities, rates, food, transport and other costs. As by the force of an involuntary wheel, people have to keep working in order not to fall foul of their never ending hand to mouth monthly commitments. Most cannot freely disengage from this merry go round of life which at the same time is unable to afford them any 'surplus value' as defined by Karl Marx to significantly improve their quality of life. It is the capitalist way of life. Some say it is sometimes akin to chasing one's tail.

And so when bereavement befalls a family or an individual, people in their droves are often on hand to pay their respects, share sympathy and offer all the support expected of good Catholics or a dignified community. But within this environment there are severe time limitations that prevent people from being around to stay and offer compassionate support as they have to maintain their shift cycles and keep an eye on the all-important end of month pay cheque. The impact of all this appears particularly harsh on the womenfolk. They have carried the child in the womb in the case of their own children. When your child has been taken away, it does not matter whether it is 5 days, 5 years or 45 years. The pain and the loss remain fresh as ever. The fathers feel the pain and hurt too. But I wish to follow the thread with the mothers. A physical part, literally a part of them is gone.

The community around, very often the source of strength and support sometimes unwittingly perpetuates the pain in the bereaved colleagues. A few expressions made with intentions to offer support that I came across: *"I am really sorry that you still feel this way. I know how you feel."* No you cannot possibly know how I feel because you are not in my situation. Sometimes people comment, *"So it has been 5 years since the little one went. I believe you feel better now as time is the great healer."* No, that cannot be correct, he/she was my child and what I had is gone, forever. Everyday is as recent as the day I lost my baby. Others innocently comment, *"You are doing better than I expected, you are doing really well."* No I am not, I am dying on the inside and I do not wish those who helped me look after my child in the final stages to feel they are responsible for my loss……And you are being judgemental again!

"You seem very calm and are managing really well." Others say, *"She is fully over it now, look at how much she sings and participates in the church Liturgy."* No I am not managing well. I am simply trying to cope with what is going on inside me. *"Sometimes when I am asleep, I meet my son and we play the old games and chase after each other, as of old. When I stretch my hands and call his name so we go back home I wake up and find it was only so near and yet so far. It was just a dream. And when I go to work or meet others socially, they have no way of understanding what pains and torments I go through with instances such as these."* The pain from the way a parent lost their child for example sudden death, road accident, long protracted and painful illness of the child cause never ending pain and a heavy feeling of loss. Others have suffered a difficult break up in relationship shortly before losing their child. This is an example of some the deep deep wounds carried by sections of the community. Fr Munyongani faced these members of the community too. He faced these realities in the daily execution of his work. Journeying with people who encountered bereavement takes time, it is not a quick fix. That journey is one that is best enveloped by prayer and immersed in the mercies of the Almighty. This adds to the context of the role this priest played in journeying with his flocks. Some wounds are the visible ones we see on the outside but the deeper ones are the invisible ones on the inside which no one other than the carrier is aware of. And they cut deep. It is the work of the good shepherd to walk

alongside the flock in these circumstances. Sometimes having to be in front to show the way. Sometimes following behind to ensure that other limping ones are not trailing too far behind. It is always a matter of reading the situation and picking the appropriate purpose.

3   Working With Other Clergy

During Fr Munyongani's time 'the glorious phase', he always seemed to draw priests in the country for one reason or other to come and participate in community worship. Some were Zimbabwean student priests at various stages of progression towards the priesthood and belonging to various Religious Orders in the UK. The young trainees would always join us for monthly community Mass celebrations. It was clear Fr Munyongani had a special place in his heart for these young men. He would offer prayers for them in the celebration of the Eucharist and publicly recognised their presence in the congregation at the start and end of each Mass celebration even when they did not have any roles to play during the Mass. He would also do the same with any Religious Sisters attending Mass with the community. The father figure Chaplain.

There were also fully trained priests who from time to time would be sent for post graduate studies in the UK by their Bishops back home. He would encourage us to seek them out as soon as they arrived and together, we would visit them at their resident parishes. To meet them in their abode and extend to them a hand of welcome to the community. On a few occasions after visiting the new priest, we sometimes identified a need to assist the new arrival with some material items. Such task would normally be forwarded to the Men's Forum to action. The identified need might be a few items of warm clothing or other accessories to make the life of the new priest a little bit more tenable. The new priest would, their timetable at their resident parish and their university workload permitting, join the community at the next community Mass: seamlessly being embedded into the community.

Henceforth the new priest would form part of Fr Munyongani's 'team'. Community Masses were occasions of prayer but even more than that, occasions of immense joy and socialisation of the community, including the community's shepherds. The newly arrived priest would team up with fellow priests to concelebrate the Holy Eucharist. As was typical of Fr Munyongani, he would usually ask the new priest to deliver the Homily, humorously telling the community,

"Today I have asked Fr Thomas (or other priest available) whom you know to read the Gospel but the Homily will be given by the new ploughshare (badza idzva!) and I want you to listen very carefully, so that when you go to stand before God you will witness for me that I provided you with a variety of experts to preach the Good News. And you must not then tell further lies but admit to God that you were well provided with able preachers. So Fr, havo vatenderi venyu (Fr here is the Congregation, they are now at your disposal!").

Having thus been 'inducted' into Fr Munyongani's team, these priests would subsequently help out with Small

Christian Masses, or they might attend with him or be sent to provide guidance to Guild meetings and celebrate Masses at such events. They would also be sent to celebrate Masses in the other Centres of the Chaplaincy as part of their role to help shepherd the community, such brotherhood and charity. These actions were not lost on us in the community. Fr Munyongani preached to us the Word from the Holy Scriptures, but he was very effectively preaching to us by his actions in the way he treated his fellow brothers. By these actions the student priests felt appreciated and were given an additional sense of purpose in what might have been a challenging phase away from home. They were able to connect and find family and friends in the Chaplaincy community. The student priests were able to share in the community joys such as weddings, birthday celebrations, anniversaries but were also able to share and experience the community's sad moments like illnesses, bereavements and counselling difficult situations such as domestic disagreements between husbands and wives, or between parents and their children.

The third group were the priests coming only for periods of just a few weeks to a few months visiting friends and family, usually in the summer. Between 2008 to about 2012 it was not unusual to have the monthly London Centre Mass with 5, 6 or even 7 priests concelebrating the Holy Mass with the Chaplain at certain times of the year. It would have been quite easy for the visiting priests to simply come over and maintain a quiet profile and not go out of their way to interact with the community.

The main reason fellow priests rallied around him was to be found in his person. A welcoming, happy and hugely prayerful priest, Fr Munyongani was much loved and respected by all the Clergy. All these brothers and sisters of our Chaplain were always afforded opportunities to integrate into the community so they could minimise their own loneliness in a foreign land and have an opportunity to make friends and practise their ministry among their own people. It was also an opportunity for the Clergy and Religious to witness the familiar unique Zimbabwean Liturgy abroad.

The priests visiting our community at various times would testified on their departure how enriched they would have been made by the opportunity to minister to the community and how the time with the community had strengthened their own faith, taught them lessons about their fellow people living away from home and how they had seen the very existence of the Chaplaincy playing such a pivotal role in keeping our people together. The Clergy and Religious being embraced by the Chaplaincy community would be invited to people's homes and sponsored to accompany the community on pilgrimages abroad and helped with accessories for their studies. All these largely through the catalytic role played by the Chaplain networking within the Church. Such unmeasured love, as St Alphonsus Liguori would have remarked.

4   A Pastoral Visit with Fr Munyongani
4.1 A visit to the newly established Huntingdon Centre

It is August 2008 exactly two months after Fr Munyongani first arrived in England as Chaplain, he is due to travel to a new Centre that he is to open where the faithful meet regularly and to mark the occasion he will celebrate the first Zimbabwean Chaplaincy Mass for this fledgling community. Things do not go according to plan and in the end no transport is available to enable the new Chaplain to travel to Huntingdon in Cambridgeshire. after the Sunday Mass at my own local parish Fr Munyongani is on the phone.

"Could you please help me as I need to get to the new Centre at a place called Huntingdon. If you are able to come and your wife is agreeable for you to come, I would be happy to assist with your fuel costs. The trouble is I do not have any idea where it is or how long it will take me to get there. The faithful are expecting me there today."

My wife does not mind. I go and pick him up, hoping to save the situation. We travel to Huntingdon a place I have never been to myself, getting caught up in heavy Sunday traffic and only arriving long after the scheduled Mass time! This community's hopes of their very first Zimbabwean Mass with the new priest have just drawn the short straw. They do not know who to blame. The Chaplain is new and could not have reasonably been expected to find his way there on his own. I am an unfamiliar face from a different Centre and the only reason I may have come could only be expected to be a work of charity. The Huntingdon faithful are grateful that I am playing the role of good Samaritan and that the new priest is finally with them.

The agreeable and good nature of the Zimbabwean Catholics takes over. Soon the group of about 30 gathered here at the local church breaks into song and drums solidify the rhythm, percussions rattling away melodiously, Zim Catholic style. Fr Munyongani and myself and everyone joins in in prayer and song. He explains that it is not necessary to celebrate another Mass as the host parish priest had already thoughtfully done this when it became apparent the Chaplain's arrival was seriously in doubt. He reads from the Holy Gospels and gives a Homily followed by a blessing. True to Zimbabwean tradition the community has come prepared with food (sadza) and vegetables, several beef stew, pork and fish dishes. The drinks come too, and we are all made comfortable. There is enough of everything to go round, and more. Fr Munyongani comes face to face with Zimbabwean hospitality in England. We are hungry (….for both faith and food) and with a sense of mission accomplished we feel we deserve what this generous community is laying on for us. After the meal the community wishes to form a committee of lay faithful and what better opportunity than in the presence of the new Chaplain. I am elevated from visiting parishioner/chauffeur to being the returning officer, perhaps more because I am an uninterested third party with no conflict of interest, rather than any profound skills in implementing democracy. All ends well and a new committee is birthed here. Huntingdon Centre is ready to roll. On our way back to London after what seems like a long day, Fr Munyongani gets a call from a lady whose mother recently died back in Zimbabwe and asks if she could have Mass celebrated at her house in remembrance. We detour to this place and eventually celebrate Mass. It had been completely unplanned. The next day Monday is a working day for me, but this is rather a small matter as I get an early preview into what would be a busy life for our Chaplain. A priest who is unable to say no to his people and community requests, both planned and unplanned come thick and fast.

4.2 A Family Memorial Mass

Some two months later on a Friday evening we take off to go and celebrate a house Mass at Margate near the English port of Dover, the gateway to France and mainland Europe. Neither of us know where this family live. Driving out of London late on a Friday afternoon has its hazards as the traffic is always so congested. Eventually we arrive at the family home after taking three and a half hours to travel 65 miles only to find the family had also invited another Zimbabwean priest--without telling us. We could have saved ourselves this arduous journey, particularly as Fr Munyongani will be on a 200-mile train journey to Manchester in the north west early tomorrow morning. Other members of the extended family have been drinking while waiting for "Fata" (the priest). There are no other parishioners of the Catholic Church in attendance at this Mass. We celebrate the Mass with me and one or two others acting as the Liturgists. I double up as Mass server and

Reader -in addition to my other role as driver. But in fact, I had a very special role in all this. I am a companion, confidante, and as we travel on these journeys we pray. We talk. We discuss current political events at home and in England. We share general talk, banter. Bonding. Trust. Love. Confidence. Exchange of ideas. Sharing opinions. And so on.

After Mass we are offered a meal by the family and sit around and share conversation. The other members of the family, the ones who had been drinking prior to our arrival then disclose that they are all baptised and confirmed Catholics and it is the reason they had wanted a Catholic Mass for their late mother's memorial. They are happy this has been done. They had never believed much in the Zimbabwean Catholic community in England. They say their views have just been proved wrong and would from now on come to the community Masses. This did happen and from this family we were to have one of the most committed members of the Zimbabwe Catholic Men's Forum. It seemed in the end it had in fact been God's intention that we visit this family so that lapsed members would be shepherded back into the fold. This little town near where in the South Eastern border town, is close to where St Augustine of Canterbury made his entry into pagan England many hundreds of years ago. As at Huntingdon a few weeks previously, the unmistakable footprint of Fr Munyongani was making its assured strides into the Mission for which the Zimbabwe Catholic Bishops' Conference had so carefully selected him.

Arriving back in London at the Presbytery about 12.30am, a few short hours before he takes off again all the way to Manchester for two days of meetings and celebrating Masses and other priestly duties with the faithful in the North West. At his front door a local destitute man appears and asks "*Fr do you have some money for me to buy food?*" When Fr responds he does not have any money and it is quite late, the man effortlessly jumps over the presbytery boundary wall which is over 2 metres high and lands into the cemetery on the other side and disappears. I wait until Fr has locked his door before I drive home. A day in the life of a priest.

4.3 One of numerous practical homilies: Bishop Munyongani preaches development projects to his congregation 2017

"Sezvamanzwa kuti vatenderi vanotambudzika, vakanga vachitoti hapana chitsva. Saka iko kuno kuparish tinofanira kuti tiwedzere tione kuti vanhu vachembera vanenge vachizochengetiwawo sei. Uye tinoda kuti tiwedzerezve sekuvaka panogara mastudents edu eCatholic kuti vawane accommodation. Ma statistics anoreva chaizvoizvo kuti huipi nohurwere hweshura matongo huri papapa. UZ chaiyo haifanani naizvozvo, NUST haifanani naizvozvo, Masvingo haifanani naizvozvo, Africa University iri kwaMutare haifanani naizvozvo. Huori hukuru huri papapa. Saka tinofanira kuti tiidze tichengedze vana. Saka kana pafungwa sezano rakadaro, panofanira kuvakiwa pokuti vana vanogona kugara. Vanogona kuchengetwa namaSister, namaBrother, vachiona kuti vanopinda chikoro vechibhadharawo mari yeresidence asi vachigara hupenyu hwakanaka. Nokuti ndovatenderi vedu vamangwana. Asi vanenge vari muhwaya yeMambo Press. Huye Ivo vana baba vanogara vepaMambo Press vachionawo kuti zvinhu zvakamira zvakanaka. Navana Sister vachiona kuti vana vagere zvakanaka.

Asi vana baba navana Sister vari voga pasina parish council, hazvigoneki. Inenge iri project yeSt Mary's Senga. Kuti zvinhu zvimire mune zvakanaka. Hatigoni kuvaka matumba. Panofanira kuvakwa dzimba dzinogudzikanwa kuCouncil. Naizvozvo zvinhu zvose izvozvo zvinofanira kuitwa nomwero, nomazvo. Asi chero zvakadai handinyunyuti ndinotenda ndinofara zvikurukuru. Ingorambai muchitsungirira zvikurukuru.

Baba Rubaya vanokusimbisai vachiti ivai nePasika yakanaka. Ndichavaudzavo kuti ndaona chaizvo chaizvo uye ndawana kwakati pfakapfaka kuzara. Saka ndinokumbira kuti murambe muri vaKristo. Vanababa navanamai murambe makashinga musaodzwa moyo nenhamo dzapano pasi. Gore rino igore rakashata chaizvo nepamusana pezvakaita nyika uye nokuti mvura haina kunaya, hakuna mabasa. Asi hatingarasi moyo, vakuru vanositi haurasi mbereko nokuti wafigwa. Saka tinongoramba tichiti, "Panguvaaa yokutambudzika, Mwarri, inhareee, Mwari inhare yavakaruramaaa, Mwari inhareee….yavakarurama…" Gungano rose rave kuimba ngoma ichidandauka, hosho dzichibvumira.

"As you have heard the faithful are struggling and going through difficult times with no respite. As a parish we need to plan and strategize so we can provide and look after the elderly in our

community. We also need to think about providing facilities like accommodation for our Catholic university students who are our future. The statistics speak for themselves and make very grim reading. Immorality and the AIDS pandemic are widespread in the community of students. The moral decadence surpasses other institutions of higher learning such as the University of Zimbabwe, The National University of Science and Technology in Bulawayo, the Africa University at Mutare, or the Great Zimbabwe University at Masvingo. So we have to go to great lengths to look after these young people. And if we agree this is the right thing to do we have to make plans to build good and safe accommodation for them. They can then be looked after by the Religious Sisters and the Religious Brothers who will then see they attend classes and have dignified accommodation and pay for this accommodation to retain viability. This whole project would need to be built in a secure enclosure within the Mambo Press grounds, the Catholic printers.

But the priests and the Sisters cannot implement such massive undertakings on their own. It has to be a partnership with the parish council of the laity. All the works have to be projects of the St Mary's Senga parish. We have to be professional in what we plan and build. We cannot put up slums, our buildings must be approved by and be to council standards and specifications. And with all that we have so far achieved, I am satisfied and am very grateful for efforts made by all of you. I encourage you to persevere and keep moving forward.

Fr Rubaya sends you all his best wishes and prays you all have a blessed Easter. I will tell him in return that I came here and found a packed Church of enthusiastic parishioners. Please remain in Christ and do not be discouraged by the setbacks of this world. This year has been particularly harsh, with erratic and inadequate rains, rising unemployment and other hardships. But we should not lose heart. Our elders gave us the sage advice that, "You do not throw away the child carrying straps because you have suffered a miscarriage." We have to continue to in exhortation, (and, characteristically he breaks into song, the famous funeral song, "In times of troubles and tribulations, The Almighty is the guide and sentinel, ... The Almighty is the guide and sentinel.......of the faithful forthright...... He is the guide and sentinel of the faithful and forthright....."

The congregation spontaneously and wholeheartedly join in with their bishop, complete with thunderous drums and percussions. The end of one of those powerful sermons. And the Holy Mass proceeds from The Liturgy of the Word to the Profession of Faith and prayers of the faithful. The congregation has once again been taken to a stratospheric level of prayer and reflection. This is what typically happened at each of his celebrations of the Eucharist. Every single word straight from deep in his heart. Sweating as if from a steaming house. Serving the Lord. Unmistakable hallmark desire to provide for others each time preached The Word: - the Gospel in action.

4.4 Fr Methuli Lanele Moyo on Sekuru Munyongani

The setting is a meeting of priests in the presence of Bishop Bhasera. A young priest Fr Methuli Lanele Moyo recounts on a video clip that has gone viral his encounters with Bishop Munyongani whilst he was a deacon and just about to be ordained into the priesthood. It so happened that Sekuru Munyongani was presiding over a meeting of the St Joseph's Men's Guild.

Bishop Munyongani asks for the young deacon to be brought to him. The young deacon, somewhat unsure of himself and what this might be all about presents himself to the Bishop who promptly instructs him to settle down,
   "*Pindai pindai. Garai zvenyu apa.*" (Come in come in. Sit right there sir.")
"*Zita?*" ("Name?")
"*Methuli Lanele Moyo*"
"*Taurisa, taurisa!*" ("Speak up, speak up!")
"*Ndinonzi mudeacon Methulialele Moyo*" ("I am Deacon Methuli Lanele Moyo".
"Unogona kuverenga here?" "Can you read?"
Sekuru produces an H-Metro (local) newspaper from some bag which presumably someone must have given him in his resident town of Gweru. I read the article given me.
"*Unoziva chinonzi scandal here?*" ("*Do you know what a scandal is?*" he asks in a rather impatient loud voice")
I mumble a response, already sensing this is not going well at all.
"*Unoda kuita mupriste here?*" ("Do you want to become a priest?")
"*Hongu Sekuru*" ("Yes, your Lordship")
"*Hino ndinokugadzai sei mechiita zvinhu zvakadai? Huh!Taneta nazvo izvi*" ("So how can I ordain you when you do things like this? Huh! We are tired of these shenanigans!")
"*Mechidambura moyo yavatenderi kudai? (I am not going to ordain you!*" "When you are ripping the hearts and souls of the faithful like this! Tell me how can I ordain you as a priest? Well, I am not going to ordain you!") I try to mumble that

the person responsible for this scandal is not me, but this does not wash with Sekuru Munyongani. He asks me to leave and call the senior priest who had told me the Bishop had wanted to see me. After a long while I am eventually told that the preparations for the ordination would proceed. But I have gone through difficult patches.

Before the ordination, on a different occasion another incident occurs. I am still a deacon and helping Sekuru to prepare the altar for a big open-air Holy Mass in the park. Some of the chalices need to be covered but we have nothing to use. During such Eucharistic celebrations, a veil is often used to cover the chalice to prevent dust and flying insects from coming in contact with the bread and wine. Often made of rich material, the chalice veils have not only a practical purpose, but are also intended to show honour to vessels used for the Sacrament. Well here in the park we do not have the luxury of such a veil. Sekuru says to me, "As a person who has studied Theology you need sometimes to improvise". He tells me to use some purificators. A purificator is a white linen cloth which is used to wipe the chalice after each communicant partakes of the Blood of Christ. We get the job done and all goes well. On a different occasion we have a similar open-air Mass celebration and Sekuru is present. As the enthusiastic deacon who was already admonished for not covering chalices from the elements, I happily place purificators on all chalices.

Sekuru comes and sees my handiwork, and furiously comes to me and says,
"What is this?" I get a smack and a telling off. "Do you not know what purificators are and what they are used for?" It is wiser not to say it is you who told me to use them for this

purpose the last time to prevent dust and elements from settling in the chalices. I am confused and disappointed. Tears stream off my eyes despite my best efforts to hold them back. Some weeks or months later the big day of my ordination arrives. On the occasion I was ordained 5 times. "*Ndave kukugadza vatenderi vose vechiona. Mudeacon uyu wakatora nguva zvikurukuru kwazvo wechigadzirira zuva ranhasi. Zvino wagona Methuli mwana wamai vangu*" (With his hands on my head. "This deacon has taken longer to reach ordination preparing himself to this special day. Methuli, my mother's son you have done well."). We are friends again after all.

"*Asi hatidi kuzonzwa kuti hatichakuoni iwe wagadzwa, nokuti taneta nazvo zvemisikanzwa!*". (But we do not want hear in future that you have sly manners and often cannot be found when you ae needed, because we are tired of errant behaviours from the Clergy). Oh dear oh dear…
And in the end, I was ordained and here I am.

5   On Pilgrimage with Bishop Munyongani

The Memorandum of Understanding (MOU) establishing the Zimbabwean Chaplaincy in 2008 was signed by the Zimbabwe Catholic Bishops' Conference (ZCBC) represented by ArchBishop RC Ndlovu and the Archdiocese of Westminster represented by Cardinal Murphy O'Connor. It expressly stipulated as one of its provisions that the Zimbabwean Catholic faithful had an obligation to go on pilgrimage at least twice a year as part of maintaining and deepening their faith. One place specifically mentioned was The Holy Shrine of Our Lady of Walsingham in East Anglia.

This local Shrine designated the Nazareth of England is one which is accessible to anyone in the country and so there would be no excuse not to visit.

Visiting Holy Shrines on pilgrimages and Retreats were some of the spiritual activities which Bishop Munyongani would speak himself hoarse while encouraging the Zimbabwean Catholic faithful to undertake. In fact during some of his Homilies he would hold out the MOU to the parishioners telling us that what he was telling us was one of the pillars of his work that the Bishops in Zimbabwe and England had jointly mandated him to champion as our Chaplain and that if we did not heed this we were not only disobeying him, but disregarding the directives of all the Bishops and ultimately what God expected of us.

As was typical of him, he would always lead us by example on these. He would lead on local pilgrimages. He would urge Centre leaders and Guilds to arrange Retreats and encourage their members to go on pilgrimages. In 2011 he led a group of over 150 young people from around the Chaplaincy to The Holy Father's World Youth Day (WYD) in Madrid, Spain. Knowing his passion for pilgrimages parishioners often invited and sponsored him to lead their pilgrimages to Holy Shrines such as Lourdes, the Holy Land, Rome, Malta etc.

Bishop Munyongani had a particular passion for the Holy Land where Our Lord Jesus was born, grew up and was ultimately crucified for the salvation of all of us. He would lead annual pilgrimages to the Holy Land and these pilgrimages often included non-Catholics who preferred to join the Catholic pilgrimages led by Sekuru Munyongani, because of the prayerfulness of those pilgrimages. I was fortunate enough to go on two of the pilgrimages to the Holy Land that he led. I remember very clearly that as we departed from England Bishop Munyongani would be the usual person we all knew. As soon as we arrived in the Holy Land you would almost think that you were now being led by a different person. He would make a declaration on arrival in Israel,

"We have travelled a long distance to be here and we left everything that we were doing. Many people do not have the same opportunity to be where you and I are now. This is the land Our Lord Jesus Christ walked and was crucified for you and me. We have not come on holiday, or tourism, or to eat good food. We have come to pray and to atone for our sins so that we may receive God's mercy. Abraham was here, Jacob was here, King David was here. And all the prophets and great people in the Bible. So, we have to be serious."

This airport de-brief might be repeated later if it appeared the pilgrims were forgetting why they were in the Holy Land. And woe unto you if it appeared you continued to flagrantly disregard his exhortations to behave on his pilgrimage! At each site that we visited, he was always well prepared and would know the Biblical verses which would be read at such places followed by giving an explanatory Homily and blessing before we moved on. But one always needed to manage his time keeping to ensure we departed the hotel on time. Visiting holy shrines was always serious business for him. Many colleagues have confirmed too that as soon as Bishop Munyongani arrived in Israel, he became a different person altogether. He always reminded us that a pilgrimage and a tourist visit were totally different things which must not and could not be confused with each other. And we were on pilgrimage. He would brook no time wasting or distracting activities such as taking pictures or shopping while we were visiting sites. If you attempted to do so, you could regret your actions when he admonished in the strongest terms, in public. At Bethany one vendor who was trying to sell us handbags when our instruction was to head straight to Mass from the group coach was left holding two ripped up pieces of one his bags! He did not look kindly on vendors trying to sell their wares to his pilgrims if this was distractive. A Bishop on a mission!

"I will bring them to my holy mountain and make them joyful in my house of prayer. Their burnt offerings and sacrifices will be accepted on my altar, for my house will be called a house of prayer for all the nations." **Isaiah 56:7**

This is what Bishop Munyongani wished us all to become. His approach to spirituality captured his views on the sanctity of his ministry: zero tolerance for any acts defiling or disrespecting anything to do with prayer.

6   Concluding remarks

Every human being is created in the image of God. We live on this earth for a finite period of time and our faith teaches us that we should take the gift of our lives as a grace mercifully given by the Lord in His infinite mercy towards mankind. We experience good times, we experience bad times. Sometimes in these difficult moments we begin to believe we are being punished for some past transgressions of our forefathers. Or we see the lives of others as so blessed and rosy compared to the short straw that we ourselves have drawn. Or go further to even curse God for the inadequate package that He has given us. There are also times when we are more inclined to want to pray and express our gratitude to God because things happen to be going well for us.

But the reality which we often forget or choose to ignore is that "*……in all things God works for the good of those who love him, who have been called according to his purpose*". **Romans8:28**. And, "*…………He is from all eternity one and the same. Nothing can be added or taken away, and He needs no one to be His counsellor.*" **Sirach42:21**. What we have to do, no less, is to love and honour God. We add nothing to Him when we praise and worship Him, He is always the same. He does not diminish when we boycott or get angry with Him. He does not depend on us in any way. But it is us who are enhanced when we pray and keep His commandments. It is not a bargaining or quid quo pro relationship with the Almighty where we would get this if we give Him that. Sirach tells us that God needs nothing from for His wellbeing. St Paul however assures us in Romans that God will look kindly and not forget those who look up to Him and serve Him. He is mercy itself.

We have to live our lives taking each day as if it was the last so that should He come calling we would be ready and good to go. "*But know this: If the homeowner had known what time the thief was coming, he would have stayed alert and not let his house be broken into.*" **Matthew24:43**. These are some of the many messages the late Bishop Xaverio Johnsai Munyongani was so relentlessly trying to communicate to his flocks using every armour in his huge spiritual arsenal to preach The Good News. He did not tire or lax in his duty. The numerous testimonies attached give their own accounts of the personal and other observations made by a wide cross section of the faithful who encountered him. And all of them testify that their own lives and those of their loved ones were immeasurably changed by their interacting with Bishop Munyongani. As for me I find that on every count when God called him, his job here on earth was done. The lingering question is, when He comes calling at your door and mine, will your job or mine here on earth be done? Amen.

Appendix 1: THE TESTIMONIALS

BY THE CLERGY

The Most Rev XJ Munyongani: The faithful servant of God: Fr Elias Chinzara STL

First of all, I want to express my deep and sincere filial love to my Formator, the Most Rev X J Munyongani. I will never forget him as a Formator for seminarians at Chishawasha where he stayed perhaps for more than a decade. I first met "Mhofu" as he was popularly known, before I even decided to go to the Seminary and this was at a Diocesan Conference at Triashill Mission in Manicaland. I must have been about 14 years old at the time. When I saw him, I loved him because of his clarity in speech, precision and high sense of humour. Being a youth at the time, I started imitating the way he spoke in my own presentations and felt like going to the seminary. My second meeting with him was at the Regional Major Seminary of Chishawasha in 1992, my first year of Philosophy. I spent a decade with him in the seminary, during which time I felt his paternal love, immense concern and goodwill in my formation for the Holy Priesthood.

However, the priesthood is defined as *'in persona Christi capitis'*, meaning, 'in the person of Christ The Head'. Or rather, priesthood means 'mediation' between God and man. In other words, the Holy Father, the Bishops and priests participate in the priesthood of Christ. The High Priest is Christ Himself. The idea of the Church as an instrument (*Lumen Gentium 1*) remains active in our Ecclesiology. Therefore, there is no private priesthood, but it remains with

Christ Himself and for the people. Looking at the person of Bishop Munyongani, I think he was a faithful disciple or priest of Christ. Looking at his person as a teacher, you could feel his passion for the Church. Hence, *'sentire plene cum Ecclesia'* (DH2880), meaning *'to feel with the Church'*. This calls for faithful's love for the Church.

Therefore, the teaching of the Church on the Bishops as the sacramental image of Christ the Lord (Christus Dominus) is well manifested in Bishop Munyongani. Hence, the person of the Bishop is important for a true understanding of the mystery of the Church. His passion for the young priest reveals the salvific mission in the midst of the redeemed human race. It is true that Christ invested the priests and Bishops with The Holy Spirit (cf Mt.28:20).

Looking at our situation in the seminary at Chishawasha, he was a model of the priesthood. In actual fact, he loved his vocation. Watching him in this situation, we too as seminarians started to love the priesthood. Perhaps most of my classmates or fellow seminarians made it to the Altar. Among them are Bishops R Nyandoro and R Mupandasekwa.

On the one hand, Bishop Munyongani was a no 'false praise', but rather just deserved being elevated to the office of Bishop. I think he did not believe in false praise. One of his potent weapons was the virtue of humility. He was such a natural or down to earth personality. Humility is the most feared virtue by the devil. The same humility makes Our Mother Mary so powerful and feared even in Gehenna. He was just a humble priest of God who loved his vocation, the Church, and ministry. He could speak about God with confidence. He spoke passionately about Jesus Christ, the Church and the priesthood. As a young seminarian, I loved him because of that. Naturally as young seminarians, we felt and behaved like all priests before they are ordained.

Another point to mention here is that Mhofu could also get angry with seminarians! But he never lost his high sense of humour and did not stay angry for long though because he prioritised his vocation as *'In persona Christi Capitis (Sacramentum Caritatis Pope Benedict XVI)'*. He knew that he was carrying a powerful name, that of Jesus Christ, the Head. He was nicknamed a 'Real catholic Priest'. That alone made him a special Formator. In fact for 14 years he offered his all his efforts for the formation of priests in Zimbabwe.

Furthermore, when Mhofu was the Dean of students, and I was the master of Ceremonies the only rule was that we had to be present at all meals and prayers. He worked hard in and out of the seminary, but always found ways to be present when needed. He therefore discharged well his ministry of presence. As seminarians he gave us the opportunity to grow and to be responsible seminarians.

I can without hesitation, confirm that Bishop Xaverio Johnsai Munyongani was a fine and faithful priest, who loved his Church, his people and his ministry. May he continue to rest in peace.

Fr Elias Chinzara STL

MY PERSONAL ENCOUNTER WITH BISHOP XAVIER MUNYONGANI: Fr. Tirivashoma Gilbert Chibira

It is my greatest honour and pleasure to have this opportunity to put down my own personal experiences with the late Bishop Xavier Munyongani upon the request by Mr Foroma who is currently based in England and is compiling a booklet on the servant of God the late Bishop Munyongani. Honestly these few pages will not be enough to put down all my experiences with Bishop Munyongani but l will definitely put down some of the experiences. I worked so closely to Bishop Munyongani both when he was still a formator in the Regional Major Seminary at Chishawasha near Harare and when he became my Bishop in the diocese of Gweru. It was indeed a unique experience and l learnt a lot from the late Bishop Munyongani.

My first encounter with the then Fr. Munyongani was in 1998 when l joined Chishawasha Regional Major seminary. I had heard of this powerful preacher full of jokes but had never seen him personally so it was one of my greatest expectations when joining the seminary to see this great man. Just on the day we arrived he was there to welcome us to the house of formation. The first impression l got of Fr Munyongani was that of a very serious headmaster and taskmaster who took no nonsense from anyone. But the moment he started to speak this whole idea evaporated. Surely, he was such a humble man full of humour. He cracked one joke after another until all the seminarians began to shout MHOOFUUU!! MHOOFUUU!! which was his totem. By the time he told us to go to bed personally l wanted him to just go on and on. He explained the life of the seminary so vividly giving a lot of examples which left us in stitches. It was thus I fell in love with this man from day one.

For the next eight years Fr Munyongani was my formator and lecturer teaching us liturgy. All his lessons were full of life, and no one could afford to nod off during his lectures. He always emphasised on the sacredness of the Sacrament of the Eucharist and the seriousness called upon to us as future priests. I remember very well the story he always told us that when you are a priest or deacon who has gone to give Holy Communion to the sick to make sure you handle the Communion with great respect and deference. He gave us the example of a priest who would put the pyx with Holy Communion in the back pocket and pass through a bottle store to buy a drink. He always condemned such behaviour and he would ask us, "*Does this priest expect people to be genuflecting at his back in honour of the Blessed Sacrament. Why does he not go home put the sacrament back in the tabernacle then go to the shops?*" Fr Munyongani was a great lecturer and so passionate about the subject of Liturgy. The other thing we enjoyed as a class was how he would always forget where he had left off in the previous lecture! This was due to the fact that he was teaching all the four classes of Theology so at times he would forget the topic he was treating in his last lecture and just continue from where he left with another class! And students would always shout, "No Fr we were not talking about the 'models of the Church' (one topic he loved so much), but we were on the "Fathers of the Church" and he would seamlessly switch to that topic and proceed. Honestly l would always look forward to the lessons of Fr. Munyongani.

In my final year at Chishawasha seminary l had a number of opportunities where l would go out with him to give retreats in different parishes across the country. He is one man who could be called to any part of the country to give a retreat and he would deliver. He had the great gift of spoken languages, he could speak Ndebele and Shona perfectly well. He is one of the very few priests l know who travelled across the country preaching, and giving retreats to various groups. After my seminary training we remained in touch and we would meet regularly on different forums and he is one person who would always be welcoming and sharing jokes despite the age difference that separated us.

The next close encounter l had with Fr Munyongani was when he was appointed the Bishop of Gweru by The Holy Father Pope Francis in 2013. We received the news with great joy because we knew the man coming was a true shepherd and the majority of us priests from Gweru diocese (and any diocese for that matter) were his former students. I was privileged to be the chairperson of the committee which was organising for the Episcopal ordination of our Bishop elect Xavier Munyongani. The ordination went on well and was well attended. It clocked the highest attendance especially of priests. Mkoba stadium was full to capacity with a lot of singing and dancing. The family of Gweru diocese received their new shepherd with great joy thanking Bishop Bhasera for the work he had done as our erstwhile Apostolic Administrator. This day was marked with the famous words of now Sekuru Munyongani that "*handina rimwe bhaibheri randichavhura kana imwe verse yandichavhura isina kumbovhurwa……*"(there is no new Bible or verse l will open that has not been visited before). These words were received with a lot of applause from the

People of God gathered for this special event. Our new Bishop believed in the continuation of the Church taking over from where his brother Bishops had left off and continuing with the same work. This was really proved in his 4 years of episcopacy in Gweru diocese.

As a Bishop one of the most striking aspects l learnt from my encounter with Sekuru Munyongani is the aspect of humility. He is one of the most humble persons l have ever met in my life. He is one person who would always want to defer to others, as if he was the least in any company. As a Bishop he associated with all people: the rich and the poor, the young and the old. His attendance of funerals left an indelible mark in Gweru diocese. He would always refer to himself as "...*is hedu vana bozhiwa*..." (a phrase signifying the lowest person in the society). I can confidently say sekuru Munyongani was a humble servant of God with whom all the people of God would not fear to approach

As a Bishop of Gweru Sekuru Munyongani resembled a perfect example of a father figure. He was well known for his sermons and powerful teachings on faithfulness both in marriage life and priesthood. At ordinations he would not mince his words when it comes to faithfulness in keeping the vow of celibacy. At an ordination in Ascot after l had preached he also took the opportunity to instruct the newly ordained priest that as he is coming to join his brother priests he must not come to add on the number of scandals but must come in to be an exemplary priest. The saying of the day was .....*taneta nadzo nyaya idzi*.... (we are tired of these issues/shenanigans) referring to the scandals befalling the Church. He really expected the best from his fellow priests and always encouraged us to thrive for holiness. One of his teachings on priesthood was "priesthood is not for boys, it's for real men and being a man does not only mean putting on trousers because even women today put on trousers as well."(at Chiginya House in Kwekwe 12.10.2014).

In the four years he was Bishop of Gweru Sekuru Munyongani literally visited all the parishes in the diocese and was available at the different congresses for different guilds. He always gave great teachings encouraging people to always have in mind that we are not in this world forever so we must always aspire for heavenly things. Hence the famous song *tivavarire denga* (let us strive for the reward of heaven) would always wrap it up. I always hear the echoes of his voice saying "…*denga haripindwi ne favour nderekuvavarira*…." (meaning heaven is not a question of favouritism but it's something we must work for). Every time he canted this song the whole crowd would arise and sing along. Sekuru Munyongani was well known for singing during his Masses. At one point l counted the number of songs he sang in one Mass and they were 26. We would always joke with him after Mass that today you sang more songs than the choir and he would laugh and say "…*toda kuti zvimwirire vana baba*…." (we want the message to sink in my dear priests).

After two years of his episcopacy in Gweru diocese Bishop Munyongani asked me to go for further studies in Rome. I tried to give excuses so that l would not go but he was adamant and said this is not all about you but it's about the Church. With such powerful words l had to go for further studies but would always keep in touch with him over the phone with him giving me encouraging words always especially when l complained about my difficulties with the

Italian language I was learning. His encouraging words were always "…..*shingawo bhoki mabhonzo anopedzwa nevamwe*…." (paraphrased as 'fortune favours the brave). I always looked forward to occasions to meet Sekuru Munyongani after my studies but God had other plans. In October 2017 the final day of Sekuru Munyongani in this world arrived he was called to the heavenly home. This was really a dark cloud for Gweru Diocese and the entire Catholic Church in Zimbabwe.

Gone is the humble man of God, a powerful preacher and a hardworking Servant of God. May he continue to Rest in the Peace of God.

Compiled by: Fr. Tirivashoma Gilbert Chibira

TESTMONIALS BY THE LAITY

Bishop Xavier Munyongani: Mr Samuel Nhavira

My first encounter with Bishop Xavier Munyongani was in Zimbabwe in 1996 at St Johns Church in Emerald Hill, Harare. On this day, Bishop Munyongani received a number of women who had chosen to join the Marian Guild to promote their spiritual enrichment with a special devotion to Mary, the mother of God. He gave a touching and moving homily covering the expected roles within the parish and community of these newly received ladies. It was clear to me then, that I was listening to a man with a unique gift from God.

My next encounter with Bishop Munyongani was in 2011, when a group of Roman Catholic and Methodist Christians organised a pilgrimage to the Holy land in Israel. On our very first day in Israel, a member of our group received a message from London that her husband had suffered a stroke and she had to make arrangements to go back to London. We were told that there wasn't much hope and the chances of her being able to see her husband alive by the time she got back were very slim. Bishop Munyongani arranged a Holy Mass to pray for the lady's husband, and asked for God's intervention. The lady managed to make arrangements to get back to London and was reunited with her husband. With God's grace, the husband outlived Bishop Munyongani. Bishop Munyongani made it a point to visit the husband on a regular basis. This is a miracle that I witnessed with my own eyes that demonstrated that Bishop Munyongani was a true servant of God.

I was not the only one who sensed the power of God in Bishop Munyongani, all the pilgrims felt the same sense of holiness in him. Roman Catholics and Methodists alike would go and ask for blessings from him. There are many examples that demonstrate the nature of Bishop Munyongani in my own experience but I will only relate one more.

Bishop Munyongani was in Sheffield and heard that a man he didn't even know had passed away near where he was visiting. He went to the house to give his condolences and ended up leading the funeral service for the man though the deceased was not even a Roman Catholic and the priests from the man's own church were present but they were happy for the Bishop to take the lead role. Clearly, everyone present realised that the man had a special gift from God. His homily and his singing in the praise of God brought everyone nearer to God.

Bishop Munyongani was indeed a true man of God.

Samuel Nhavira

Sekuru Munyongani: Mr Joseph Goredema

When our Lord sent out his disciples, he told them, "*Whatever house you enter stay there until you leave the area*" Luke 9 vs 4. This was Sekuru Munyongani whenever our community Mass was in Northampton he would come and stay with us. The whole Goredema family enjoyed his teaching and humour. In 2008 I was elected the National Treasurer and was working directly with Sekuru Munyongani who was our Chaplain at the time. From the onset he made it clear financial matters regarding the Zimbabwe Catholic Community in England and Wales were my responsibility. This made our working relationship a very cordial and professional one. Sekuru and I worked well as a team to ensure transparency and accountability were key and all Centres understood that.

Sekuru was a great liturgical teacher who would make sure that correct terms are used when it comes to Mass. I remember vividly Sekuru fondly correcting me for saying "wine" instead of "The Blood of Christ" as it was after consecration. His was very welcoming and professional at the same times. Sekuru taught me a very important lesson how as a father I should always bless my family using the

Numbers 6 blessing given to Moses. Sekuru said it was crucial for a father to lay his hands on his family and invoke this blessing often for the protection of his family.

I worked with Sekuru Munyongani for a number of years as the National Treasurer for the Zimbabwe Chaplaincy in England and Wales, it was a challenging and demanding as we set up structures but the support from Sekuru made the task manageable due to his relaxed but professionalism. It was such a blessing to have known Sekuru both on a personal and professional level. Used to cherish the days he would come to our place and sleep over awaiting to celebrate a Mass with the Northampton Community. This gave me the opportunity to tape into is massive wealth of scripture knowledge and understanding of moral issues. We established a very good working relationship with Westminster as they deemed the Zimbabwean Chaplaincy to be well organised and the best managed Chaplaincy.

It was such an honour to have known Sekuru Munyongani and working with him very closely for the establishment of the Zimbabwe Chaplaincy in England and Wales. Sekuru Munyongani was a man of great wisdom whose teachings I will ever cherish.

Mr Joseph Goredema
Inaugural Zimbabwe Catholic Community in England and Wales Treasurer

Bishop Xavier Munyongani: Mr Mavelos Madimu.

In my short Christian life I have met and worked with many priests and men of honour, but none that compares with the late Bishop Munyongani in humility, love and compassion.

My first encounter with the Bishop was in 1998 in Kwekwe at St Edwards Parish when he was leading the Parishioners in an annual retreat. It was a retreat that changed my life and many others'. His presentation is still vivid in my mind and I can still picture him loading chairs on his shoulders one by one until he was unable to walk, illustrating how we weigh ourselves down with bitterness because we do not want to forgive. It was a life changing encounter for me and it was then that I became serious about going to church.

  I did not get to know much about the Bishop until fifteen years later when he came to UK as Chaplain of Zimbabwean Catholics in England and Wales. At the time that he came I was Leicester Centre chairman and Vice Chairman of the National Executive Committee (NEC). This gave me an opportunity to work closely with him and to get to know him better. When he found out that I had worked as a Headmaster in his rural home area of Chitsa in Gutu we became even closer. I will for ever cherish the time that we had with him in the UK.

His humility and genuine love manifested itself in the way he interacted with the Community. He respected everyone regardless of age or gender. He always took himself as a child servant of the people. I remember the times when we always tried to get him to attend our NEC meetings and he would always humbly say, "Do not worry about me just go ahead and I will go by whatever you agree on". He would never shoot down any ideas that came from the people. He was frank, but humble in all his dealings with the Community members.

He was a true shepherd who cared for his flock in earnest. The moment he learnt about any member of the Chaplaincy not feeling well, he would straight away go to see and pray for him or her, regardless of how far the person was. The same happened when there was a Gut bereavement or if any member of the community lost a loved one. He was not bothered about formalities or protocol, he just got on with had to be done.

When it came to celebrating Mass, the Bishop was truly gifted. He was a gifted singer, charismatic preacher, and spiritually gifted teacher. He had the special ability to combine preaching and humour without losing the spirituality of the sermons. He will be remembered for many of his famous quotable quotes by most of the members of the Zimbabwean Catholic Community.

Here is a man who could truly say, "*I have fought the good fight, I have finished my course, I have kept my faith: henceforth there is laid up for me a crown of righteousness, which the Lord, the righteous, shall give me.*" **(2 Timothy 4: 7 - 8)**

May his soul rest in eternal peace.

Mr Mavelos Madimu.

Recollections and reflections on Sekuru Munyongani: Mrs Annie Kapungu

My first encounter with Sekuru Munyongani was in the mid 90's back home. He came to our parish (St Gerard's in Borrowdale, Harare) to lead us in our 1 day Retreat as Chita CheHosi YeDenga. That was the first time I heard him speak about "*Kunwa Mujoza*". His favourite song that day was " "*Mwari wangu ndanyudza midzi murudo rwenyu*" (I embed my roots in your love, my God).

I remember him as a very practical person who knew how to defuse awkward/emotional situations. Once he managed to correct a parishioner who had spoken harsh words in full view of others. I was then the leader of Zvita (All Guilds Council) in England and Wales that time. He never discussed the issue with me although I was the victim of the irate parishioner.
He practised fairness. A parishioner yearned to receive Holy Communion after changes in her private life. He asked the parishioner to come and confirm with me as one of the leaders present, if she was happy to follow all the Church's regulations. I repeated the church teachings and told the parishioner to go back and be blessed.

That was his main practice - "*Imi vatenderi ndimi munozivana*" (You the faithful know one another better and so you can give me good advice). All he wanted was a witness for this blessing to go ahead. In 2013 he came from London to Oxford when my husband was hospitalised, to pray for him. I was humbled since he used his own resources to travel all the way and back.

I used to try and speak to him about stopping his smoking habit - it was a struggle!! *"Makuva ese ari pa Barcaster (Highfield Cemetery) akanyorwa kunzi fodya here amai"*? (He would sarcastically, Mother are all the graves in the cemetery in Harare marked that their occupants died of smoking habit?)

At his consecration as Monsignor at Gokomere Mission in Masvingo, he was blessing people who had lined up (the queue must have been between 50 and 100 metres long). In the hot sun, tired and sweat running down his face he was blessing and praying the faithful one by one on his big day. After observing this for a long time, I decided to take the drastic measure of dragging and guiding him away to have lunch and a break following what had been an extremely long day. He could not deny them the blessing regardless of the effect on his health.

MHDSRIP

Mrs Annie Kapungu

Good bye my brother
(In memory of Bishop Munyongani)

The agony that came through me
The taste of salty tears, that dribbled down my face
The sorrow in my heart

The tears, the weeping, the pain,
Some may say I didn't know him that well
So why should I cry? But, I say, I cry but not for long
I know that he wouldn't want me to

Now I sit and talk,
Memories flood my mind, The agony has gone like magic
All that's left now, is to feel the joy and
Knowing that you indeed have gone to Heaven

I wish to make it to Heaven
So, I will be at the right hand of God the father
And the left hand of you. So, know I think
The wonders the tears and the sorrow that I felt
were all just a blur. An oil less lamp if you will
Now you are everywhere
But also, nowhere watching and listening to me
There is nothing else to say but good bye my brother

© **Kumbirai Katema** (11)

Inserted by Benjamin Takavarasha

UK-based Catholic Chaplaincy Mourn Bishop Xavier Munyongani

(As published in the Masvingo Mirror, November 2017)

Rt. Rev Bishop Xavier J Munyongani

Following the death of our former Chaplain on 15 October 2017, the Chair of the ZCCEW Mr Norbert Tsvangirai issued the following message of condolence:

"On behalf of the Zimbabwe Catholic Community in England and Wales, I want to express deep condolences to the Munyongani family, all religious and parishioners in Gweru Diocese, the ZCBC and indeed the Zimbabwean Catholic Community in Zimbabwe at large, the latter deriving from how he was loved and revered by Catholics across Zimbabwe's eight dioceses from anecdotal evidence. In conveying these condolences I would emphasise that we as a Chaplaincy are, needless to say, also very much in mourning as he had become part of our family as it were, even after leaving us to be the fourth Bishop of Diocese of Gweru in 2013. The news of his death on Sunday 15 October was received with deep shock and sadness and many are still struggling to come to terms with his passing. He became our first Chaplain following his appointment by the Zimbabwean Bishops in 2007. Zimbabwean Catholics in the UK are a microcosm of Zimbabwe being drawn from every region and diocese, but he managed to gel us altogether as one family. Partly as part of the grieving process, people have been exchanging his sermons and humorous and pithy quotes in social media, with many changing their profiles to feature either pictures of themselves with him or just him alone which attests to the fact that he had touched the lives of many in a very personal way. At his episcopal ordination on 14 September 2013, apart from the official delegation from the Chaplaincy's leadership, were many who went on their own steam. This has been repeated more recently at his funeral, which incidentally was featured by the BBC. He is also mourned by many outside the Catholic

Community judging from the condolence messages we have received. Bishop Munyongani was also highly regarded by the Catholic hierarchy in England and Wales as partly borne by the fact that when Pope Francis was elected in 2013, of all the African Chaplaincies in the country, he was the only African Chaplain interviewed by the BBC to give the African viewpoint on the new Pope. A painful void has been left in the hearts of many in the UK Zimbabwean Catholic Chaplaincy. **Eternal rest grant unto him O Lord, may he rest in peace."**

Norbert Tsvangirai, NEC Chair, Zimbabwe Catholic Community in England and Wales

His Deputy Mr Conrad Masiiwa was part of the official representatives from the ZCCEW who flew to Zimbabwe for the funeral, and in his slot as one of the speakers (which incidentally was aired in part on BBC TV) at the funeral echoed in part his Chair's condolence message. As part of his speech, he conveyed the condolence message of the UK Ecumenical Men's forum Chair, Dr Paul Matsvai, who is of the Baptist Church. The full speech by Mr Masiiwa is covered elsewhere in this issue by Mr Mathew Takawona who heard the speech first hand at the funeral.

Lastly on Saturday 28 October, a Memorial Mass for all ZCCEW centres is being held for Bishop Munyongani in Leicester where further eulogies will certainly be expressed.

Collated by Benjamin Takavarasha

Bishop Munyongani as an icon of Humility, simplicity and humour by Mr Kizito and Mrs Cecelia Hakutangwi
Jeremiah 1:5 *"Before I formed you in the womb, I knew you, before you were born, I set you apart......."*
When Mr Joseph Foroma asked me to write something about Sekuru Munyongani the above scripture quotation came to my mind. Indeed, before Sekuru came to UK for

Chaplaincy duties I had known him for 4 years. This is the bit I am privileged and qualified to write about.

We first met at Chishawasha Seminary to do Philosophy and Theology as part of priesthood studies. I started Philosophy in 1967 and Xavier started his Philosophy studies a year later in 1968. Thus we knew each other for solid 4 years. This is when I first came first face to face with the qualities I am writing about: of innovativeness/creativity, humility, simplicity and humour. To Xavier all those who were ahead of him during the priesthood studies were duly addressed as vana Mukoma (elder brothers), giving them their due respect. He had a passion of doing things differently and not unreasonably holding onto "As it was in the beginning is now and ever shall be, world without end, forever and ever amen!"

In the game of football he was an impenetrable fullback during that time. With another colleague a full back as well, used to say "If you miss the ball don't miss the person what humour!"

He believed in transparency, fairness and integrity. He admired my innovation and boldness during my time at the Seminary. He had very little respect about the then traditions at the Seminary "As it was in the beginning …… for ever and ever". Examples of these traditions were Seminarians going catechising in the neighbouring villages and farms around the Seminary on foot and going without lunch boxes. The Seminary Rector expected the Seminarians to walk and to be fed by the community or families they visited. I frequently challenged these traditions during meetings and calling for change such as the use of bicycles and going with own packed lunch boxes as this would free our time to cover a wider radius and see more families. The Rector then was not amused by my suggestions. Little did I know that there was another seminarian who would report my innovative suggestions to the Rector. Fortunately the Rector when he called me to his office and challenged me about how he came to know about what I had suggested he revealed the name of the person who had 'betrayed' me. The Rector shocked me when he remonstrated with me. "He said I should be careful. Why should I make it my business to enlighten people (seminarians) who do not want to be enlightened." Xavier is one of those who used to give full weight and support to the challenges I presented to the Rector of the day. Sadly this led to my demise: first of being sent for probation for one year after I completed my Philosophy in 1970.

The seminary never arranged where I should go for this one-year probation and left it to my devises. I was blessed to get a research job at Harare Referral Hospital to do research into patterns of diseases referred to this hospital. The Seminary having found out that I had established myself at Harare Hospital fearing I would be tempted by nurses and student nurses to abandon my priesthood studies. I challenged back and said if that happened that would mean I was not of the mettle to become a priest. So I continued to complete the research assignment successfully.

I went back to the seminary in 1972 and completed one year of Theology as a sung hero from fellow seminarians and some members of staff for having been resolute to successfully complete the probation and come back to continue with my priesthood studies. I had proved the

Rector wrong in his prediction that I would be tempted at Harare Hospital and not come back to the Seminary.

A week before going back for second year Theology I got a letter to say I was not fit to be a priest and the main reason was that I was too vocal and challenging the traditions of the established order. "As it was in the beginning … for ever". Monsignor Munyongani during his Chaplaincy in the UK was very fond of this expression implying things needed to change to newer perspectives and approaches.

This is why he was very innovative in his approach to his Chaplaincy. Examples are "Men's Forum in the UK "The Dam model" an inclusive approach with all kinds of fish "men" in it and encouraging people to go on pilgrimage to the Holy Land.

We took him on his very first pilgrimage to Malta which he greatly appreciated. From this he joined a Methodist group as an individual to the Holy Land.
There after he was the main crowd puller of the mainly Catholic pilgrimage group organised by Catholics from Zimbabwe based in UK known as "Image Travel" that organise each year pilgrimages to the Holy Land for Catholics and non-Catholics. They have earned the reputation of being a "ministry in the field of evangelisation" not only to the people who live in the UK but from the diaspora and straight from Zimbabwe.

PERIOD OF CHAPLAINCY ENGLAND AND WALES

His salutation/greeting us each time we met was "Hesi or Hello Mukoma Hakutangwi or Amaiguru Hakutangwi in the case of my wife. We often protested and said "Sekuru tava nevana nevazukuru venyu" (We are now your children and grandchildren) and do not deserve to be addressed as Mukoma or Amaiguru Hakutangwi. He insisted that his ascendancy to the priesthood, Monsignor and finally Bishop (Sekuru) was secondary to the fact that our roles preceded his ascendancy to his roles ." This is humility and simplicity at its best.

We had also the privilege of going to the Holy Land for 4 years in a row 2013 to 2016 with the late Bishop Munyongani. I was once tasked to awake him up every morning so he could prepare early to meet the demanding tight time schedule for the Holy Shrine visits of the day. He would humbly express gratitude for my tasks/efforts of waking him up each morning due to his increasing frailty and failing health to meet the targets of the day.

On three occasions: on the boat ride in the sea of Galilea, the Church of The Transfiguration Mount Tabor and at St Peter's Primacy Church overlooking the sea of Galilee while in the Holy Land, Sekuru became so moved and emotional three times and shed tears appealing for prayers to strengthen him in his pastoral responsibilities in the Diocese of Gweru, another sign of humility and simplicity in his efforts to shepherd his flock. This echoed his earlier fears when he was confirmed to become the Bishop of Gweru. Like our Lord Jesus at the Rock of Agony in Gethsemane Sekuru had pleaded to be exempted from taking up this post in preference to continued Chaplaincy which he had successfully championed and trail blazed and was executing to near perfection. When approached and asked "Chii chirikunetsa Sekuru" (What is the problem?) he would surprise the questioner by his response" Heya! zviya zvinonzi Mwana asinga chemi anofira mumbereko" "Ini handidi kufira mumbereko". (They say a child who does not cry may be ill and die in the mother's baby carrying shawl. I do not wish to die in that shawl!) Bless his great humour but always with deep spiritual meaning and messages.

Another strand of his simplicity is that he often said to be a "Sekuru" or a priest does not mean they know it all. Each one has things which the other does not know. We must respect the views and expertise of each other and learn from each other. He often said priests or Bishops have lessons to learn from the laity. Sekuru you inspired us ! Help us to emulate your example! We remember you fondly!

Mr Kizito and Mrs Cecelia Hakutangwi

Sekuru Munyongani: Mrs G Mushayabasa

In the early eighties, I studied at one of the Pope's universities in Rome at the same time that Bishop Xavier Munyongani was a student in Rome. He was then a young vibrant priest.

What I remember remarkably well during my time of study in Rome was that when The then Rev Fr Munyongani was the main celebrant of the Zimbabwean Mass in Rome, we all went for that Mass expectantly, excitedly prepared so much for a lively touching Holy Mass.

We got so much from his friendly welcoming manner, and his deeply profound witty homilies, which left us reeling with laughter to the point of almost chocking. The thing is that he could illustrate any point he wanted to drive home from the scriptures in very expressive examples from our background as Zimbabweans. He had so much wisdom, it was unbelievable.

I got a pleasant surprise when here in the UK we were told that we had a new Chaplain. I first saw him at a sad occasion of the requiem Mass for the late Fr Andrew Chigodora, and very much like him, he hammered it into us that, "*I tell you that anyone who gives you even a cup of water in my name because you belong to the Messiah will certainly not lose their reward.*" (Mk 9:41)... and he went on to stress that surely Fr Chigodora must have given such to many, and that to God, Fr Chigodora was a champion in his servanthood. This was very assuring to us all.

From then on, I was very expectant of our Chaplaincy Masses, and sure I was not disappointed. He had become more seasoned in his homilies."*Tese takanwa kamujoza*"... story illustrated so effectively to us that we all have sinned and have fallen short of God's grace. But not without painful ribs from the laughter that the story drew. He himself, was very respectful, humble, friendly, loving, dignified, accepting and very good at picking talent from his flock which he sure used for the kingdom.

He loved and raised the men's forum in the UK to a great level, he effectively promoted all the guilds, youth groups to a great height. He loved the flock, rejoiced with the rejoicing, and mourned with those who mourned. He is greatly missed.

Mrs G Mushayabasa

Xavier Munyongani- The Evangeliser and True Minister of God Full of Catholic Wisdom: Mr Godfrey Mahaso

1. Background
I knew Bishop Munyongani way back from Zimbabwe before he came to United Kingdom in 2008. All the time I knew him to be:
Caring, compassionate, understanding,
friendly, humble, merciful. A Confidante. Approachable- You would not hesitate to go to Confession with him. I believe he was chosen by the power of the Holy Spirit for the sake of the good of the people of God.

2. Liturgy / Homilies
In the United Kingdom, parishioners get fidgety once liturgy goes beyond forty five minutes. This was never the case with Bishop Munyongani's liturgy. He caused parishioners to laugh a little, cry a little and ultimately feel very good about themselves.

Bishop Munyongani's homilies provided insight into the meaning of the scripture and related to the lives of the parishioners he led in mass celebrations. He never read them from the notes and showed everyone present in church that he was an expert at his subject and that he invested a lot of time in preparing for the sermons. Every mass he celebrated was inspirational.

3. Awareness of the Parishioners' Expectations
Bishop Munyongani was aware that no matter what he said or did, some parishioners will be upset. Because of this, he had a big heart to embrace everyone in his quest to proclaim God's mission to become reality within the wider

community, not only of Zimbabweans but to all parishioners wherever he celebrated mass.

4. Bishop as a Visitor at Our Home
Our family hosted Bishop Munyongani almost every last Saturday of the month between 2009 to 2012. He was a good visitor. We felt very free to speak our minds out in his presence. He prayed and celebrated mass in our home. He ate and drank what he was offered but never enjoyed beans sighting that this more of boarding school relish. Upon request, he celebrated a wedding mass for our daughter Tinashe Thelma. When our mother passed on, he celebrated a funeral mass at our homestead in Chirumanzu back in Zimbabwe.

5. Football
Bishop Munyongani was an ardent supporter of football. He supported Barcelona Football Club. HIis favourite player was Messi whom he nicknamed "Simbi Dzinodya Dzimwe" He used to send me messages to record the football games and in his language told me "VaMahaso mufushe bhora ndigozoona ndasvika
Mr Godfrey Mahaso

Bishop Munyongani: Dr Paul Matsvai
Bishop Munyongani, at the time that I first met him was serving the Zimbabwean Catholic Community as Monsignor Munyongani. He was a man of humility though he occupied an elevated ecclesiastical position.

He, along with Commissioner Makina of the Salvation Army, who at the time served as Africa Secretary of the

Salvation Army, and Evangelist Mutema of the United Baptist Church were among the earliest pioneers of the Zimbabwe Christian Men's Fellowship UK, a responsive assemblage of Zimbabwean Christian men who resolved to come in fellowship across denominational frontiers.

As this was a new initiative, it required the active support of all participating leaders at the highest level. The late Bishop Munyongani, then Monsignor Munyongani, surprised me with his open door policy from the time the idea was mooted. He, as **Paul said in Galatians 2 verse 9** gave me and others who were initiating this fellowship the right hand of fellowship as he made time to meet me in his parsonage in North London.

Over a cup of tea that he had prepared, we had a wonderful time of fellowship and sharing together the vision for fellowship across denominational lines. Not only did he endorse this initiative in his capacity as the serving leader of the Catholic Community but he was the first to liaise with both leaders of the Catholic Men's Fellowship and the Mothers Union which at the time had already birthed the Mothers Mubatanidzwa. The right hand of fellowship was also realised as the late Bishop Munyongani liaised with Mr Foroma, the then Chairman of the Catholic Men's Forum and Mr George Chapwanya who at the time served as the Secretary and was also to become the Inaugural Secretary of the Zimbabwe Christian Men's Fellowship (ZCMF) at its inception in 2010.

With his full blessing, the Inaugural Planning Meeting of the ZCMF was held at Pastor Gobvu's house in Milton Keynes and in attendance from the Catholic Community were Messrs Foroma, Chapwanya and Mrs Dube, who was the incoming Mubatanidzwa Chairperson. Bishop Munyongani's encouragement energised many to break virgin ground in this fledgling association that saw the birth of ZCMF as a result of a number of planning meetings in which the leadership of the Catholic Community gave the right hand of fellowship.

It was not in any way surprising that at the Inaugural ZCMF Conference attended by well over 120 men in 2010 in Milton Keynes, that the then Monsignor Munyongani was fittingly given the privilege of being the Keynote Speaker. The Theme of that defining Conference was *'Let us arise and build'*. In his presentation he emphasised for a holistic approach to building in those areas that would make Zimbabweans strong and productive as a nation. These areas that required building were spiritual, economic, political, social and also building enduring families at the personal level.

ZCMF thus sought to address these areas in subsequent Conferences and one offshoot has also been the creation of the Zimbabwe Diaspora Network UK, a civic platform that seeks to proactively engage the challenge of national development by mainstreaming the Diaspora as key stakeholders in enhancing national development.

In all these endeavours, there has been a realisation that the time for lone wolves who think they can provide answers to national imperatives on their own is gone. There is thus a crying desire to establish synergies across denominational and party lines and evolve a holistic model that addresses national challenges from a vantage point of unity. Indeed,

Bishop Munyongani was a voice that gave practical impetus for Christians to be proactively engaged with those issues that can make a qualitative difference in people's lives.

May his soul rest in eternal peace after a life of service well lived to glorify God in all his endeavours.

Testimony on the late Bishop Munyongani written by Dr Paul Matsvai Inaugural Chairman Zimbabwe Christian Men's Fellowship UK

THE LATE BISHOP XAVIER MUNYONGANI: Mrs A Bere.

We speak of canonised Saints in the Catholic Church yet there are some who are not recognised in our human eyes, I would like to take this opportunity to express how this well loved and respected man deserves to be amongst those deemed Saints by many. I am sure my sentiments are shared by many however, at times many go unnoticed.

Bishop Munyongani is most probably remembered for his courage to speak up in public for what he believed to be true, a true servant of God. The Bishop was much appreciated and loved by many before even his death. His voice lit up the church and his profound Homilies touched a lot of people of different denominations and not just Catholics. He is also remembered for his energetic and lively presentations during Homilies, enthusiasm and had an approachable personality, a man who embraced everyone, and was always ready to serve others rather than be served himself. I remember on several occasions when we would beg him to rest when we noticed he was not well even when there was evidence of being ill; swollen legs or hands, he would still go out and humbly do his work passionately without complaining or seeking attention. A true devoted man of God, that was Xavier as a priest or even after being sworn in as Monsignor or after being consecrated a Bishop. I would like to say "He had an open hand policy" accommodating anyone who needed to see him.

St John Vianney quote- *"You either belong to the world or wholly to God"* The Bishop used to say *"you can't love both Money and God,"* in our vernacular language ("Mari or Mwari"). He made individuals realise or made us aware of our responsibilities or consequences of our actions; and was always very direct and to the point.

He was a good listener, non-judgemental, humble, full of humour, cheerful, a great adviser, counsellor, loving, the list is endless but most importantly he was full of zeal to work for the Lord. It appears he knew that he did not have a long life ahead of him hence his dedication and passion for his work- he never wanted to rest and would ignore efforts from those who cared and loved him to rest as he continued to labour in the God's vineyard. Also his last homilies/sermons were mostly focussing on eternal life and he had made himself well known by the song "TIVAVARIRE DENGA" and he would sing happily this song wherever he went and has a lot of quotes that he is now known for and many use them frequently which as though jocular always made sense and formed a major part of his teachings.

Majority of us feel robbed by the "Heavens" by his "untimely death, but I am sure the same Heavens gained a Saint. He seemed to have endured silently a lot of pain as we came to know of his diagnosis. He is missed as the gap he left is irreplaceable. We trust he still continues to pray for us even in his next life.

May perpetual light continue to shine upon him, and may he rest in peace. AMEN.

Mrs A Bere.

Sekuru Munyongani was the most humble person I ever met: Mrs C Mutemachani

Sekuru Munyongani was the humblest person I ever met in my whole life. Though never hesitant to call a spade a spade he was so respectful, very approachable, accommodating, full of humour and was always there when his flock needed him. He would always find time for anyone, he did not bog himself down in protocols or procedure when people needed to contact him. Anyone could call him directly at any time. And when called at a time he was unable to pick the phone he would always apologetically return all calls and attend to his people. He wouldn't even say come pick me up he would use public transport when making pastoral visits to parishioners.

He was selfless, even knowing very well that he himself may be unwell. He would always regularly check on me to ask about my poor health, not considering himself. He was more concerned about my health than his own. He never called me Mrs Mutemachani he always called me Mhamha (Mother) and he related with my children as mukoma Tapiwa, mukoma Tawanda & Sisi Betty even though they were at ages of possibly being his grandchildren had he been a married man rather than a priest. He treated me with such respect that if he got annoyed with anyone whilst we were on pilgrimages, and if I approached and talked to him to calm down he would listen and behave like a little child to their own mother. Such respect. He was so grateful in every little thing you did for him.

He was very rich spiritually and his trademark was to preach in parables and jokes using stories and anecdotes related to real life situations. His teachings were very powerful. Sekuru Munyongani treated every individual with respect irrespective of their religion. He really loved going to the Holy Land and we used to travel to the Holy Land each year even when he had returned to Zimbabwe ss Bishop. I remember one occasion we went on pilgrimage and he was poorly, struggling to walk with swollen feet and hands. I asked him to take a break the following year so as to rest and regain his strength, but he said to me "bodo mhai basa raMwari harizororwi. Tichanozorora tikaneta taakumakuva tichishaya anotipindura". (No Mother, we do not take respite from God's work. We will rest all we want when we are finally laid to rest in the cemetery).

I could go on and on and on. I really cherished the time we spent with him and I thank God for his life. Rest in peace my son, dear and faithful servant of God. Indeed, you ran the race and fought the good fight as St Paul told us. You deserve the crown of glory in the realm of The Lord Almighty. Tionane nenyasha dzaMwari. (We will meet again, by the Lord's mercy).

Mrs C Mutemachani

2019/3 the late sekuru Munyongani: Mrs Eddah Gatakata

Mbuya Anna kugadzwa

We happened to be the first group kugadzwa by father Munyongani! We travelled to Birmingham in a mini bus which was being driven by my husband.
Mai Dube introduced Father Munyongani as Sekuru Munyongani! That was enough to summarise the kind of priest he was!

On our way back we had the privilege to have him on board. The first thing he did was to apologise to my husband, for not recognising the husbands during the ceremony. The sense of humour was amazing, taita kunge tapfekedza chirikadzi!
He noticed some resemblance between me and my friend Thembi Mhasvi and from that day he addressed us as twins.
I then had an opportunity to drive him to Mubatanidzwa in Southampton. When I was fuelling my car, he gave me 5 pounds. I could not take money from him. He insisted that I take the money because I did the driving! I ended up taking the money to make him happy. When I look back at that exchange I see how significant that giving was!

He was a giving person, he gave me so much not financially but spiritual!
I was ready to receive from him. He used to quote Peter from the acts of the apostle, silver and gold I don't have but I give you the spirit of God.

Workaholic

He was not one to say no to anyone in need of his services. I remember having a section mass at Mai Page's house! After mass around 21 00hrs, message came through that Mr Chiura mother had passed away. Sekuru Munyongani said he had to go and say mass.

The deceased was a METHODIST but that didn't stop sekuru from doing what he did best!

We had a lecture on how Methodist came to being and he was singing Methodist hymns.

Mai Kadeyadeya and I got home very late. Sekuru Munyongani stayed to council the bereaved. He emphasised the need for unity and supporting each other. As time went by I witnessed and benefited from that particular partnership emphasised by our Chaplain

Motor Neurone Disease (MND) diagnosis

in 2010 I started feeling unwell and having trips and falls and being clumsy! I knew something was seriously wrong, I confided in him. The amount of support I received from him was unmeasurable. He became my spiritual director who brought the new meaning of what suffering means to a Christian.

The disease was said to be terminal, and prognosis was not good. Some doctors had ruled me out. But He gave me the courage to approach the throne of grace with confidence for its only God who has the final say. He linked me up with other people who had experienced health challenges to give me hope that if god did it for others, he can do it for me.

He used to phone and visit me for one to one sessions. He would turn up unannounced just to encourage me. He said several mass in my house and encouraged me to stay strong.

At church he would invite me to the alter to pray for me. I would feel the presence of the holy spirit and I would cry unstoppable. With Time I lost strength in my upper and lower limbs.

I couldn't go to church and he will tell everyone during mass (kumba kwamai Gatakata uko, apparently he would point different direction Everytime! They would joke that we thought you moved house. His point was you can't claim to be a Christian musina mabasa) people would come and tell me they have been challenged by baba to come and visit. He would tell me kuti murikuparidza shoko makagara ipapa amayi, allow God to use you.

2013 Hospital admission Royal Free Hospital, North London

I went in for a planned procedure which was supposed to be maximum 5 days. It turned out with me staying for weeks. Father Munyongani visited me from music course. He had just learnt what became his famous song baba ndimi muzere netsitsi. He tried to teach me the song, but he was still struggling himself. Fortunately mai Rigava and Gloria came and they helped each other.
He told me about a man who had killed a soldier Lee Rigby in Woolwich. He
said his prayer is for god to give those working hands to me so I can use the hands wisely to provide for my family.

Extraordinary man

He came to visit me at home, I remember this like yesterday. I was standing leaning on my husband, as he extended his hand to greet me I managed to move my hand to greet him. Lulu my support staff questioned what happened. He didn't comment, but I went on to say the body is responding to the holy people and we just laughed.

I remember the wise words and the Bible sessions we had together. 1 Peter 5 after suffering for a little while god of all grace will restore you to your glory. That gave me hope!

Farewell visit
Due to deterioration in my health my house needed adaptations!
I had to move house temporarily. I went to stay with my sister in Romford!
Unfortunately, sekuru Munyongani came to tell me that he was going back to Zimbabwe.

He came to an empty house but I got the message from the angels. The interesting thing is I had a dream about him telling me important message. He was dancing to Mai Maria song but behind him were 2 priests!
The important message he had for me was to remain focused and not to be anxious about what the professionals might be saying to me. He insisted that I should know where I belong. After some time we had a new assistant priest who joined our local parish church.

Father Francis from Nigeria, he is the priest I saw In my dreams behind baba Munyongani! He took me under his care. Did a lot of work with me and just took over where sekuru had left.
I am yet to come across the other priest.
October 2017 I was critically ill in ICU and I woke up with a very strong conviction that sekuru Munyongani was not in this world anymore. My family and friends couldn't tell me

They thought they were keeping a secret from me. When my husband
told me after discharge in November I just said I knew! It's amazing. Kubata kwaMwari!
After his death I have seen him twice in my dreams encouraging me to pray for me to overcome. He was speaking like a prophet.
I strongly believe that he is in heaven.
What qualifies someone to be a saint?
Mrs Eddah Gatakata

Sekuru Munyongani: Mr Claver Gozho

The laity:
He loved his lay faithful. He has celebrated home masses for the sick, the dead and many with private intentions in churches and private homes. When I first met him, he gave a talk and was encouraging the lay people to remain faithful. He said the priests, religious brothers and sisters had no monopoly on holiness.

Gifted preacher:
At one time some priests would give a three-minute homily regularly during Sunday masses. This was not satisfying to many Catholics to the extent that people would question why priest training would take so many years on people who would fail to deliver the message. This feeling would change when the late Fr Munyongani had occasion to give a homily or a sermon. You would think he was the only one who was entrusted with the task of preaching whilst the majority of the clergy would administer different duties. If he gave a 20 minute sermon you feel he should just go on.

Tribalism:
He sees people as equals. After his ordination in 1977, he was posted to serve in different areas amongst them St. Alois - Gowo in Silobela, a place where there were Shona and Ndebele tribes. That was the time when Gukurahundi – a conflict war between some former Zipra forces and the Zimbabwe Government over the harassment of former ZAPU leadership by the Mugabe government. This resulted in the government unleashing a partisan brigade which was involved in the genocide of over 20,000 civilians mostly of Ndebele tribe. Silobela was one of the areas where the genocide took place. Fr Munyongani treated all his parishioners as equals and was trusted by all the his Christians.

Respect for ladies in Guilds:
He has praised women's involvement in guilds where men have lagged behind. Each time men took steps in joining guilds also requested ladies to look after his 'first years' or 'his Form one Students'.
On his mandate to tell the people about the Gospel:
He would always say he was there to tell the truth of the Gospel. If people continued to defy the Gospel, he said he was prepared to come in front of Yahweh and tell him 'I told them what you said and he had no guilt of omission'.

Values on fighting
He used to tell of a father who took his son to a pub until such time the child wanted to go home to watch boxing on television. The father still wanted to socialise in the pub when the son was asking him to take him home. It so happened that whilst the son was pestering the father a fight

broke out between two other men. The father asked the son to watch the two men fighting instead of going home to watch boxing. The father was even saying that fight was better for the son to watch because it was live. This was an example of a father was encouraging his son to value bad things like fighting.

African fathers attitude to children's boyfriends
When daughters get married in church most Zimbabwean men feel proud just like parents from many different countries. However, the problem is that Zimbabwean fathers in most instances do not want to see their daughters dating their boyfriends. Fr Munyongani would tell of a man who saw a daughter walking with her boyfriend. He just went for the boyfriend and started beating him up until he started bleeding. This was very painful for the daughter to watch. She ran away and so did the bleeding boyfriend. The daughter stripped her clothes and approached the father telling him she wanted to take her life and the father was shocked. The girl asked him why he beat her boyfriend. She was asking the father to examine her to confirm if she had lost her virginity by simply walking with her boyfriend. She challenged the father to explain how she would come to wed without first going into a relationship. She asked him to expect her to have a wedding with a tree. This has been a great lesson for some of us.

A teacher on morality
Fr Munyongani used to give teachings on morality in informal discussions with his sheep. He talked about epicureans who used to enjoy their food. They would eat and after a while would induce themselves to vomit so as to create space for more food. This was an example of a people

that believed that people would live in order eat rather than eat to live. He said God in marriage wants people to love each other, giving to each other and procreate. God would bless them with children. If people are in love and engage in conjugal acts but say they do not want the acts to give children, they are saying this time God should stand clear in their act. This is mockery to God. That is why the church takes artificial contraception as a sin.

Man of respect
He respected the Soko clan due to his aunt (his father's brother's wife) as if they were his own mother's clan. His mother was a Chuma and he respected them a lot. He would address most people using honourific plural.

Mr Claver Gozho

Appendix 2: Recalling Some Condolence Messages: What the people said

(*Although some of the many messages in this Appendix have been translated into English, many have been left in the vernacular language, in which they were given as that seems to capture the raw spontaneity of the emotions expressed.*)

* Presented here are only some, from huge exchanges of deep-felt condolence messages from the day Bishop Munyongani passed. These have been anonymised, but they capture the spirit and mood among the multitudes haemorrhaging after the sad loss of this icon. In keeping with multilingual capabilities of the Bishop himself, the package of condolence messages contain messages in Shona, Ndebele and English. I recall driving back from the Music Course with my friend with him and we had just learnt the song "*Mwari muzere netsitsi*" (The Lord of bountiful mercies"). We spent the whole journey back trying to teach him how it went but it was hopeless as he loved the song and he also had his own way of singing it! Till we meet sekuru zororai murugare (Rest in peace).
* I couldn't play it through - nyangwe zvichinzi murume haachemi, ndachema (Even though they say mature persons do not normally cry, I cried).
* Nematambudziko chokwadi. Asi kana vanga vadzimbikana zvakanyanya Musiki vavazorodza. Tinotenda nendima huru dzavakashanda: muma parish, vavakaitisa marunyararo, vavakaitira Misa dzerufu nenyaradzo, vavakadzidzisa kuSeminary, isu vavakashanda navo muno, naivo vavakashanda navo vave Bishop. Dai waro vapinda nemusuwo wedenga vachienda kumufaro usingagumi. (Sincere condolences

for sure. But if he had been in excruciating pain perhaps The Almighty has given him rest. We thank the huge swathes of the Lord's vineyard that he served, in the parishes, those whom he led at Retreats, those for whom he celebrated the Eucharist and Requiem Masses, those he taught at the Seminary, us whom he worked with in the priesthood here, and those whom he worked with as a Bishop. May he be rewarded the crown of everlasting joy in heaven).

* Thank you so much my brother, sincere condolence to you too. I was saying to my wife last night that weird as it may sound, to me personally his passing away is equal to the passing away of my own father in 2002. Sekuru has taken a piece of me with him. I do realise that he had the same impact on many people and you too included. He was perhaps an angel living in the flesh. May He Now Rest in God's Heavenly Peace.

* Good memories when I went to bury my dad. Sekuru was not happy we buried my father without telling him. His own words were '*hamuna mvumo yokuviga mutenderi wangu musina kundiudza*' (you have no right to bury one of my diocese's faithful without telling me). He was such a humble man. He took us into his orchard to eat some grapes. He was growing them. We were given our own cuttings to go plant at home so he would eat them when he visits and so that all visitors to our homestead would also eat them. I had a chance to see him and talk to him in January 2017. Rest in peace Sekuru. Am singing Tivavarire denga. Let us sing and pray.

* I was dumbfounded and did not know what to do. I decided to sing the song 'Make me a channel of your peace'.

* Got up for 3 o'clock prayers as usual but up till now I haven't knelt down to pray. My heart bleeds indeed. Just read today's Readings & sent my devotions. May the Lord grant me the serenity to accept the things I cannot change; courage to change the things I can and the wisdom to know the difference. Your will, not mine be done, Dear Lord. I surrender ALL to YOU MY LORD; withholding nothing.
* Sekuru Bishop Munyongani has passed away, it's so sad
* Ma1 chaiwo. Mweya wa sekuru Munyongani ngauzorore murugare ne tsitsi dzaMwari. (A strange occurrence, may Bishop Munyongani's soul rest in the peace and mercy of the Lord).
* Ndarwadziwa vaive mupriest wedu tiri ku high school, tinonamatira mweya wavo
* Taurai zvenyu vakoma zvarwadza izvi ini vakaviga mai vangu gore rapera
* Ah tarasikirwa chokwadi sesangano.
* Mweya wavo ngauzorore murugare netsitsi dzaMwari.
* Aaah it's a black Sunday for us Mwari mutambirewo mweya wemuranda wenyu akazvipira kukushandirai all his life. MHDSRIP.
* Mushandi waMwari chizorora hako wakakunda, wakarwisa enda uzorore. We will miss you 'ndichambono feeder matwins'!
* Mweya wavo uzorore murugare chiedza chisande chivavhenekere narini wose.
* Mweya wavo ngauzorore murugare netsitsi dzaMwari
* Aaah its a black Sunday for us Mwari mutambirewo mweya wemuranda wenyu akazvipira kukushandirai all his life.

* Mushandi waMwari chizorora hako wakakunda, wakarwisa enda uzorore. We will miss you 'ndichambono feeder matwins'!
* Zimukwende zimukwende iro zvanzi nababa sunungura zvawakatakura zvireurure."
* Tivavarire denga, denga harisi refevha asi ndere kuvavarira
* HOLYLAND WILL NEVER BE THE SAME! DAI MWARI VATIBATSIRA. Just groaning & sobbing. In my bed. My heart is heavy & very saddened. Bishop is gone. We got him a ticket for our November pilgrimage to Israel & as we speak his passport we had sent for a visa at the Israeli embassy in Pretoria.
* Sekuru Bishop Munyongani has passed away, it's so sad.
* Sad indeed. Mwari vaita kuda kwavo. MHSRIP.
* What a pity. Ngativanamatire. His sole mission in his entire adult life was to bring souls to the heavenly Kingdom. Let's pray that God's mercy, love and kindness will be on him and will forgive all his failings and accept him into His Kingdom.
* Nematambudziko vana Baba. Mweya wasekuru Munyongani nemweya yevatenderi vose vakafa ngaizorore murugare netsitsi dzaMwari.
* May his soul rest in Peace... so sad news sekuru Munyongani fambai zvakanaka nesuwo tichatevera.
* Hii vanhuwee Mwari mati tidiiko!
* Very sad indeed, may his soul rest in eternal peace.
* Ndarwadziwa mupriest wedu tiri ku high school, tinonamatira mweya wavo
* Taurai zvenyu vakoma zvarwadza izvi ini vakaviga mai vangu gore rapera.
* May his soul rest in perfect peace.

* Mwari ndimi muzere netsitsi zorodzai mushandi wenyu murugare rwenyu
* Nematambudziko maKatorike tarasikirwa MHSRIP.
* May his dear soul rest in peace through the love and mercy of God. Amen.
* Tine urombo zvikuru. Rest in peace.
* Ah tarasikirwa chokwadi seSangano.
* Mweya wavo ngauzorore murugare netsitsi dzaMwari.
* Vafudzi vedu vapera hama dzangu zvinorwadza.
* Nematambudziko hama dzadiwa tarasikirwa zvikuru.
* On a separate note but equally sad, Fr Martin Schupp CMM passed away this evening. He served as the Apostolic Administrator after the resignation of ArchBishop Emeritus Pius Ncube, before ArchBishop Alex Thomas.
* We pray for him.
* So sad may their souls rest in eternal peace.
* What a day...May his soul rest in peace.
* Oh no! May his soul rest in peace.
* Vose vakafa vari mumaoko enyu vazarurireiwooooo...Avo vose vakafa vachikumbira tsitsi dzenyu mambo VAZARURIREIWOOO DENGAAAA.
* Mwari Mambo tambirai vana venyu mugare navo misi yose . Mwari Mambo tanbirai.
* Vapeiwo zororo risingaperi Mambo.
* Aaah nhai Mwari wedu tiitireiwo nyasha MAY THEIR SOUL REST IN ETERNAL PEACE.
* Sekuru Munyongani zororai murugare. Penyu makasakura mukazunza mukapedza tichasara tichirangarira rudzidziso rwenyu. Pindai mumba menyu muzorore murugare.

* Ko zvomoramba muchindichemedza, ndinombonzwa kurwadziwa wena. This man did a lot for me zvisina anoziva mufunge. Now rest in eternal peace.... God bless your soul!
* "Sekuru Munyongani vanga vari mufudzi wevanhu for shuwa. No matter how ill he was, you would find him traveling hundreds of miles to be with vantenderi in their time of need. You didn't need to ask Sekuru for Misa in your time of need, he took it upon himself to offer Mass. Things we took for granted!"
* We will surely miss him, and may the dear Lord forgive him any transgressions and grant him eternal rest in His bossom." We will miss you 'ndichambonofeeder matwins'!
* Zimukwede zimukwede iro zvanzi nababa sunungura zvawakatakura zvireurure."
* Tivavarire denga denga harisi refevha asi ndere kuvavarira.

Eternal rest grant unto him oh Lord. May your perpetual light shine upon him. May Sekuru's soul rest in peace.

Appendix 3: Sekuru Munyongani's Top Drawer: What he himself used to say:

"Sisi hatizorore iyezvino, kana tafa ndopatozorora handiti paguva panonyorwa kunzi Rest in peace?" (My sister, we work and do not rest now. Do we not write on out epitaphs, "Rest in peace". That is when we rest.)

"Pfidza mutendi pfidza unotinyimisa mvura" (Repent, person of faith, lest the heavens withhold the rains!")

"Zvamunoti hamuna mari ko zviFoster beer munonotenga nei -- HERE?" (You always say you do not have monies for Offertorties, how come you always have enough to buy cans of Fosters lagers – why!)

"Regai ndibve zvangu pano pamunoverenga mari ndinosvutira fodya koko mungatozoti mari yedu yopisiwa!" (Let me remove myself from amongst these people dealing with cash for the Church and have a cigarette lest the faithful think their money is literally going up in smoke!")

"Munoti Roma yakanaka inobvumira doro….wonzwa zvonzi haaa zuro takanwa kuita lights out chaiko, Mutenderi anoita lights out?... here? (You say Catholicism permits partaking of alcohol and you hear this fellow brazenly bragging, ohh yesterday I was completely lights out! What cheek!)

"Ndege yevanhu yotode kuwa yakatakura zvibhonzvo zvibhonzvo zvemishonga." (Some of you travel with so much black magic powders and herbs from Zimbabwe that the aircraft almost falls from the skies under the heavy loads, due to your beliefs in superstition despite what we teach you in the faith)

"Ini Mwari ndichanomutaurira kuti ndakavaudza vanhu venyu asi havanzwi." (When I get to the Pearly Gates, I will boldly tell God that I tried all I could to teach your people, but they are so stubborn and hard of hearing.)

" Kungofa nemashift chabuda hapana" (Why do you kill yourselves doing shiftwork and yet we see no apparent or tangible outcomes or outputs?)

"Vamwe venyu ndivana 'Hunge'….Hunge nyoka…..hunge hove. Hamuzivikanwi zvamuri chaizvo." (Many of you are so multi faced you cannot really tell what they are: snakes, fish, crustaceans, wild animals. No one knows exactly what you are.)

"Muchanotongwa nemapiritsi nemishonga iyo murikutora (kuba) muzvipatara memunoshanda." (You will receive your just judgements for the medicines and pills and other items that you routinely shamelessly steal from your workplaces without a thought or remorse).

"Hamudi kuenda kurupinduko moda kuita mufushwa wematadzo…. Here?" (We offer you opportunities to go for the Sacrament of Confession, but you resist this. Are you planning to have your sins preserved as dried meat or vegetables?)

"Varume musafunga kuti kana maroora Madhuve, moti vana Madhuve vese vava vakadzi venyu. (Men should not think that when you marry a Madhuve then all ladies of the zebra totem are your wives. Your wife's sisters and cousins are relations of yours, they are not your wives too!).

"Aaaah watsunga iwe nani! Ugadzo haisi group work; iti ndatsunga kwete kuti tatsunga.... (Speak for yourself deacon! Do not say "we", say "I" have decided to dedicate my life to the Lord as priest. The ordination is an individual Sacramebt and not a group project endeavour." Sekuru Munyongani, during a Diaconate Ordination, July 2017)."

"Chingatonetsa kutema muti mukuru, makwenzi chero nemaoko todzura tichirashira kure…." (What would be more difficult would be to trim or cut down a matured tree, the little ones we just pull out and cast far away into the periphery. On the ease with which the Church would discard errant Seminarians who refused to mend their ways. Sekuru Munyongani, addressing seminarians from Gweru.)"

"Vazere vanaMother (Superior) varere kumapuranga, kwete kuti vakafa nekukura asi ne BP yokunetswa nemi munouya muchitora mhiko pano...." (There are many Mother Superiors lying in the cemetery who died due to high blood pressure and not because of age because some of you were giving them, a torrid time. Sekuru Munyongani giving advice to Religious Sisters making their final professions at Driefontein Mission).

"Zimukwende zimukwende iro zvanzi nababa sunungura zvawakatakura zvireurure" (You should go to Confession to unload the heavy burden of sins that you are carrying).

"Tivavarire denga, denga harisi refevha asi ndere kuvavarira (We must strive to reach heaven, there is no favouritism about getting into heaven. It is a privilege that must be earned).

"Ndinongofara zvangu senzira yebhazi." (I am as happy as a wide tarmac road, playing on the Shona language double meaning of the word that means both happiness and width. But more deeply reflecting his happy and easy going nature).

SHINGAWO BHOKI MABHONZO ANOPEDZWA NEVAMWE (A small dog called Bhoki is encouraged to be strong and feed and the same trough as the tough thoroughbreds lest all the food given the dogs is eaten by the big and strong. An encouragement to the faithful to persevere in the faith).

VASIKANA MUSANGOBVUMA KUITWA SEMANGO IRI PAMISIKA. WESE ASVIKA ANONGOPFANYA. (Girls do not allow yourselves the be treated like mangoes on a market stall, which any passer-by may just casually handle and leave for other customers)

"Regai maForm 1 angu awa akadero ambodzidzira" - vaireva Men's Forum tichangotanga muna 2008 kuti varume vauye kuChechi (Leave my first graders be and give them time to learn. In a light-hearted reference to the fledgling Catholic Men's Forum back in 2008 and thereabouts so they could make their tentative steps until they became sure footed and grounded people attending and participating in Church activities).

"Ramba uchiseva pasi pemuriwo pane nyama." (Perseverance rewards in the final analysis. Hard work pays off eventually).

"Tose takanwa mvura yemunjoza." (We have all sinned at one time or other, so there is no need to point accusing fingers at others.)

"Mahara akafa kwasara mukoma wacho bhadharai." ('Freebies' died a while ago, he is survived by his brother 'Pay your way'. In short there is no free lunch).

"imi zino rabva kwasara vende tsumo yavakuru." (The good old days are gone, and you have to recognise and accept the realities of life).

"Iwe unozviziva zviri mumwoyo mako huya unamate, huya unamate(singing)" (Only you know what is in your heart and what your failures are. And so, come and kneel down and ask for God's forgiveness).

" Maizara muno muchurch vanhu vakaendepi ? Mavakuita vana very nice. (You used to fill this Church and all the pews. Where did it go wrong? Where re the faithful? You also appear to be pretending to be Mrs and Mrs Nice guys,.On returning to London as Bishop in 2015 and finding the Mass attendances at the London Centre and at other Centres very much diminished.)

"Pafund raising unonzwa kana munhu asina kumbobvisa mari achiti " takanga tiripoooo ne mafata aivapoowo zvese zvakafamba zvakanaka!" (Even the parasitic and hangers on at important events like community fundraisers will declare that they were there too (ther also rans) and that they were mixing with the Clergy and the Religious and oohh yes, all went swimmingly well. And they they did not contribute even a penny but ate all the food and partook of the drinks meant for the good causes).

" Zvibvunze ugere ipapo zororo nderavatsvene" (Ask yourself what your role in the Church, the rewards of heaven are for the holy ones only. From an old popular hymn from the Protestant churches.)

" Kungorara semombe kuti bhi hapana muteuro kana munamato?" (How can you live like an animal that just feeds, and at the end of the collapses in a heap to rest to chew the cud awaiting to do it all again tomorrow).

"Imi veLondon pano vamwe vanhu makaisa kupi church yaizara iyi (remarking about low attendance)" (You London people what did you do with the other parishioners who used to fill this Church? A question Bishop Munyonagni repeatedly asked on returning to the UK in 2015.)

" Maziso tubhobho tubhobho……." (A rapid blinking of the eyes associated with some tropical animals, which folks interpreted as characterising pointlessness and lack of purpose).

" Yavanguva yeEaster ka…vana baba kana wainwa mafoster 4 worega mamwe woendawo pa2…chinjaivo maitiro." (We are now in Lent when we are called upon to fast and give Alms. You the fathers of hpuseholds, where you used to have 4 beers please cut this down to 1 or 2. Mend your ways please).

"Tarisai makokomborerwa nemafata mazhinji muno muchechi matiri asi unowana munhu asingaiti reururo…..machanotsva nazvo izvi hamheno henyu. Indai kurupinduko uko. Umo muna Baba Marizane, umo muna Baba Chiona, uko kuseri kuna Baba Magugu. Isharaude." (Please note that we are currently blessed with many priests present with us now, but still some do not want to go to

Confession. You will be sent to hell for this. Do go to Confession. You have a wide choice. You have Fr Marizane, Fr Magugu and Fr Chiona. Please go and reconcile with the Lord.)
"Vatenderi vadiwa tisati tatanga muteuro wedu weMisa, ngatirangarirei matadzo edu............ Kune vamwe varikutumira mari nemidziyo kumusha.... Kumusha uko vanzwa nokutenda, kuti vanonyora tsamba........... navamwe vachinyora nyangwe nepama WHATSAPP!.... Hanzi makaita Moyondizvo, Mhofu, Mazvimbakupa...... pasuru dzamakatumira takadziona mari tirikuiona!.....Izvo zviri zvinhu zvokuba!!!! Zvibvunzei hana dzenyu. Chawambovinga kumuteuro weMisa nhasi chii kana usingazvioni izvozvo kuti zvakashata? " (My dear brothers and sisters before we start the Holy Eucharist, let us call to mind our sins. Some are sending cars, trucks and appliances home. Those receiving the items gratefully acknowledge via letters, phone calls, Whatsapp messages thanking you by your totem. When these are stolen goods! Examine your consciences. If you cannot atone for these, then why have you come to the Holy Eucharist?)
"Huyai muite rupinduko nhasi tine mafata 4, huyai mutaure zvinhu nemazita azvo. Musangoti Ahhh Baba kudhakwa bedzi. Taurai chokwadi!" (We have 4 priests for the Confessions today. You must name all your sins individually, do not just Fr, eeeeeh being drunk. You must be explicit with God!")
" Zimukweende...... zimukwende rangu hanzi nababa, turunuraa…." (song) (A line from a song in which the singer acknowledges the massive burden of sin they are carrying and and encouraging self and others to offload through penance).
"Murume mukuru unowonekwa uchifamba kubva kumashure uko uchida kuzokanda 10 cents ko ukadonha

mukati makazara vanhu wakabata 10cents ikati ngwendere unoti kudii???" (Are not grown men ashamed to walk the length of this Church just to drop a 10 pence coin in the Offertory basket? What would you say for yourself if you tripped and the coin hit the concrete floor and rolled in front of these little children?)

" Vamwe munongonzwa kitsi dzichingochema kuti meow! meow! dzakatarira vatenderi vakananga kuMisa izvo dzirikubvunza kuti "Mweya yeyi ko iyi?"Mweya yeyi ko iyi? namabasa anopindwa nawo muno. Ndoochitendendero..... HERE??" (As some travel to Church the cat ominously cry meow meow wondering what spirits reside in the hearts of these people. Is your faith questioned even by these feline creatures?)

"Vamwe venyu vabereki venyu havagoni kunyora asi vakatengesa mombe nembudzi kuti mudzidze muve zvamuri izvi. Ikozvino munongoti svisvisvi kutaura chirungu 6 to 6. Hino vochifona kuti mwanangu mvura yonaya tutumirewo hedu yekuti titenge mbeu tirime hedu nemaoko edu. Moti, 'aaaa musadavira foni. Vanhu vekumusha vanonetsa.' Heya nhasi vava vanhu vaninetsa? Vatenderi musadaro chengetai vabereki. (Some of your parents cannot read or write but they sold off cattle and other beasts to get you an education. And now you speak English all day long and when the plead with you to send some cash to buy seed and fertilizers, you say ahh do not answer the phone, the people back home are a nuisance. Is that so, they gave everything for you and now you call them a nuisance. I plead with you, do look after your parents as good Catholics are expected to do.)

"Mai vemurume vanonzi vamwene, kureva kuti mwene wazvo ndiye muridzi wemwana vanamai." (The mother of your husband deserves respect and dignity. Please treat them as human beings).

"Kuchemera kuna Mwari hanzi ndipeiwo ndege, une airport here...?" (Some of you ask God for unrealistic things. You ask for an aeroplane as if you own an airport!).
"Zvinhu zvevanhu zvanga zvichifamba zvakanaka zvino imi mapfeka nhasi mouya kuzokanganisa . Paigamuchirwa vanamai muchita kuita ma full members." (To you who have been inducted into the Guild today, please remember that things have been going smoothly, so do not become spoilsports.)
"Kana dai mukapfeka mabhanhire maviri maviri akachinjika pachipfuva hazvirevi kuti muchaenda kudenga!" Referring to members of Joseph Guild! (Even if you were to wear two Guild sachets across your chest, it is no guarantee you will enter heaven, it is your works that matter.)
"Kunyangwe ukakonewa kupinda napamukova , ungakoniwa kupinda denga nyangwe napahwindo mai Mariya variko? Simbai kunamata Rosariro." (If you have kept the faith, if you fail to enter heaven via the main entrance, Our Lady will hoist you through the window! [On assuring that those who live well will not fail to get their heavenly reward.)
"Motorara makazvitsikirira nemagumbeze mai vako vachirara vachidziya matanda...Imi!" (When you sleep you overlap yourself with blankets and duvets when your own mother is sleeping by the log fire. Do not be so cruel to your own parents!")
 "Taneta nazvo izvi zvevanhu vanotora mhiko vasingarevesi.... (We are now tired of people who take religious vows when they do not mean it. Sekuru Munyongani at Religious Professions n Ordinations).
"Ndichakugadzai varume asi kana uchiziva kuti seri uko kuna Grace, buda pachena sa driver wetarakita tizive kuti zvakona....." (I will ordain you as priests but if yuk now that there is Grace [a girlfriend, 'small house'] somewhere, come

out in the open now, like a tractor driver and we end this process now).

"Dai varungu vaidzoka nhasi voti zvamakatora nyika makazodii nayo, tinovati kudii; ndozvimwe vakatisiira maParish dai vaidzoka voti makazodii kubva zvatakakusiirai taiti chii..." (If the white colonialists were to return today they would say since you took the country, what developments have you made, it is the same too in the Church, the early priests left us the parishes and if they came back and asked what we have done what would we say for ourselves?)

"Musamboshamisira kuti tapiwa ma certificate, hamusimi vekutanga uye vamwe vanotori nema death certificate amusati mave nawo....." (Do not brag that you have been given certificates today, as you are not the first and others also have death certificates, which you do not yet have!")

"Panoungana mapositori, usiku hwese vasina shangu vadzisiya kunze kwesowe asi haumbonzwi kuti pane ashaiwa shangu yake, asi MaRoma kubirana; kungoungana umwe washaiwa zambia umwe washaiwa mari umwe washaiwa foni; nyara Mutendi nyara!!!!" (When members of the Aplostolic faith meet overnight in vigils without lighting you never hear that anyone has missed a pair of shoes. But as soon as Catholics gather together there is always an outcry with people missing all manner of items. Why? You should be ashamed of yourselves!)

Appendix 4: Three Years On: celebrating the anniversary of his death: the grief lingers on

I read the whole piece in one sitting, without a breather, in one sitting/seating. So captivating, so poignantly presented, so "Munyongani-ish"; so full of humour but still serious – a picture of the MAN he was, the PRIEST he was; the DEEP MAN he was, the MONSIGNOR he was the BISHOP he was – TYPICAL MHOFU – OUTSPOKEN (like his sisters!!). Indeed, he was truly an amazing MAN/PRIEST/MONSIGNOR/BISHOP.

May his soul rest in eternal peace, my Brother. (On reading a mini version by myself of an anniversary celebratory remembrance article on sekuru Munyongani in October 2020).

Kutaura chokwadi, mandigonera zvikuru kuru, nendangariro dzaMuseyemwa.

Wish he was alive to go through the memories about him. Shumba, don't you think that it's a good idea to tell each other about our talents and charisms. It's like, am feeling strongly, why all this about Sekuru Munyongani when he is not there to celebrate such acknowledgements appreciations. He might have gone with a different world view, and yet the world is full of appreciation. Imagine, if the appreciations were presented to him during his life time, am sure, by now, he will be still with us, fighting to reach greater heights. Anyway, may he rest in the peaceful hands of God, whom he faithfully served. Something that touched me on Sekuru Munyongani's funeral. This was said by the Gweru Diocese Pastoral Council Chair. He said, with Sekuru Munyongani, you will not have to bother yourself going to his office, he, Sekuru Munyongani will bring his office to you. For me Sekuru Munyongani, was a Parish priest for sometime, a

Church History teacher, Seminary leader, a colleague in Priesthood, a Homeboy, and above all Sekuru Munyongani was my sekuru, as Mom's brother. Yes, he was gifted in many areas, but was not that gifted in administrative business. He was more of the outgoing Pastoral approach and less of if not lack of planning skills. He was a priest who could book five people at the same time, same venue, same everything, only to create jokes to ease down the victims such lack of planning. Without over defending his lack of planning skills, Sekuru Munyongani was too much engrossed in the belief that Do not worry about tomorrow, for tomorrow shall sort out itself. Zororai Murugare Mhofu.

Thank you very much Baba for the beautiful collection of our late Saint to be Bishop Xavier Munyongani. During his last visit to England, he passed through my house and he gave me the very same Scripture - Psalms 116. He said, Mhayi Garai neScripture iyi mumba muno. Munazoisa picture yeMwoyo Musande kuti igare Mumbai muno Mhayi. He blessed the whole house and he left.

He was a Saint that we didn't recognise, because he ate sadza like us, the Lord gave us him to see the good of Christ with blood pouring on His face due to a crown of thorns pricking His skin.

I've started invoking Xavier Munyongani's name to pray for me and intercede for me. Prayers are being answered. His soul is beautiful that we see God in him. Let us continue to pray for him so that steps commence for his beautification. Thank you, Lord Jesus, for giving us Bishop Xavier Munyongani. May God Beautify and Purify his soul. May you meet God in your Everlasting Peace mwanangu.

Great man indeed. "Sisi munoramba kupinda muchita munorambirei? Muri kanyanyonakidzwa nei kunze uko, micheka inopera" Mufudzi wakanaka who fought a good fight to the end. MHSRIP.

Sekuru was a true dedicated shepherd of the Lord Almighty and did so with great humility and sacrifice and I will always remember and cherish his words and support. The legacy he left is second to none, MHSRIP.

Sekuru Munyongani will always be remembered, for he gave great sermons indeed. May his soul continue to rest in peace. Indeed, Behold Your Mother. Well reflected. I miss him. We had this mass as he came to Zim to become the Bishop. He cried so much and said, "I told them so many reasons why I cannot be the Bishop and they would not hear of it". He said that he was told that even if he does serve 2 3 four years that would be enough. Indeed, it was to be. In those years vakasakura vakazunza. Rest in peace sekuru. So many sweet memories of you my sekuru.

Chiedza chisande chivavhenekere musande wedu in the making.

A great messenger of Christ. MHSRIP. Mai vangu (Mrs xxx) vakadzidzisa sekuru Munyongani mu Standard 1. Sekuru vave mupriste vakauya kwaMutare ku retreat vakasangana namai vangu. Vasati vaparidza vakatanga vati "Nhasi ndafara ndasangana namistress vangu vakandidzidzisa mu Standard 1." Vakavasimudza vanhu vese vakavaona. Kubva musi uyu the Catholic Church played a big part in our upbringing. My mother was known as the greatest preacher of all time's teacher. May sekuru Munyongani's soul continue to rest in peace.

Continue to rest in power sekuru Mhofu you fought your battle and won.

Zororai murugare, you have run a good race.

The best there ever was...muzotichingurawo isu musi watinodaidzwa nezwi nyoro raBaba vedu...isu anabozhiwa...

He inspires me up to now. A Bishop par excellence when he came to Redcliff l was the mission secretary by then .....Sekuru Munyongani vakataura pamusoro pehuori hwuri munyika nekuvharwa kweZISCO nekuda kwehuori kunwa mujoza ....vanhu vese vakabuda misodzi Rest in peace Sekuru a Hero of Faith.
A developer his focus was to have more catholics especially in Lower Gweru
Sekuru zororai murugare. Makatisimudza mukati imba yaMwari ivepo.
Ndinokurangarirai nerwiyo Tivavarire denga.
Hanzi 'bataiwo maverse aya nokuti ndimi sisi mukuru anenge akamirirwa kubva mhiri.Vanikwe paunonzi chitaura vaakungohwihwidza kuchema izvo hauna kana verse raungati uudzewo vanhu.' MHSRIP.
Tinokurangarirai nemabasa enyu akanaka, nerudo rwenyu, nekuzvininipisa kwenyu, nerukudzo rwenyu uye nedzidziso dzenyu dzinogara narinhi wese. Zororai murugare shava.
Zororai murugare Mhofu. Kusanzwa zvedu makasiya matidzidzisa, kusagona kukopawo zvamaitiudza tichingoti maziso tubhobho tubhobho. Tireverereiwo isu vatadzi.
Sekuru Munyanyi Handikangamwi Mass yandaka kumbira yokutenda kuchengetwa kwandinoitwa navana vangu kubva zvakandisiyana nababa vavo. Makaita Mass yakandikomborera zvikuru vana vanondichengeta zvakanaka chose hapana chandinganunyuta Mwari vakagamuchira minamato yenyu kwamuri lkoko rambai muchigotinamatira vo. lni nemhuri yangu tinemi tichitenda mabasa enyu ose amaiita pasi pano Zororai murugare rwaChristo Tenzi wedu makarwa kurwa kwakanaka Rest ln Peace.
  "Shinga Bhoki" vaidaro Sekuru Munyongani just to encourage us all.

A no nonsense man a father figure and a cultural icon whose words burnt like a furnace fire. You could judge yourself and know where you belong after his Homily. You left a great legacy to those who knew you. In the game of draughts it was to us a punishment plus a great move. May our minds always turns to what you taught. Rest peacefully for you finished your race.

We remember Sekuru Munyongani for his incisive talks especially vachikoka vanhu kuRupinduko " unoda kuchengeta zvivi wozozviitisei? Enda kuRupinduko urerukirwe."

He challenged couples to remain faithful to each other and for men to take care of their wives when sick.

He gave an example of a woman who donated a kidney to her husband vachiti dai arimurume aisabvuma kubatsira mudikani kusvika pakadaro.

I remember vachiti, 'rimwe zuva uchanomira pamberi paMwari wavekubvunzwa zvamabasa ako epano pasi, wanike wongoti maziso tubhobho - tubhobho uchingoringa - ringa.' He was so inspiring May his soul rest in eternal peace.

Ndorangarira vachitaura nezvezvivindi zvemamai zvamai vakaba nzimbe kuchiredzi vakazogezera nyaya mupurisa akasara ane mhosva zororai murugare sekuru makatidzidzisa zvakawanda musanotirevera kusada kuita rupinduko sokutaura kwenyu.

Sekuru hanzi gentleman rakarova suit. Kusimuka muchechi kundopira mupiro. Ko ukadonha usati wasvika wowanikwa murooko wakafumbata 50c kkkkkk.

Nyaya yerupinduko sekuru was ever saying hakuna asina kubatabata pindukai. Ndikangokutangirai kuenda ndinovaudza sort them. Zororai murugare sekuru mufudzi wakanaka

Sekuru vaiti...Ndikashevedzwa na Mwari....ndichavaudza kuti ndakavaudza vanhu venyu... hamheno zvenyu musingade kuterera nekuita zvinodiwa naMwari.
Then he would go on to sing " Turura katundu kako....."
I had done a project yefundraising pa Centre yanga tafamba zvakanaka chose.   Sezvinoitika nguva dzese pakawana vaitura zvavaitaura. Ndichitaura na Bishop ndakavati gore rinouya handichaiti. And then he says kwandiri.... vanhu mungavagona here? Kana Jesu chaiye mwana waMwari akavakonewa wani ....
What a generous soul, he came to see me in hospital May 2013! read a news paper article of a man who killed a solider in the street. Sekuru Munyongani said to me, amai munamato wangu if only God will swap his hands with yours.you can use them wisely.(I lost strength in the limbs due to illness.)
During Mass at Driefontein I think it was burial Mass during consecration he said Abraham and Isaac went up the hill and left the servants at the foot of the hill maboora ngoma akasara pasi saka kwiraiwo paGomo nesu nguva ino inoera kana uri boora ngoma hameno hako.
Rest in peace sekuru so missed and so loved.
We cannot thank you enough for the example and encouragement you gave us through just being "you". Makaunza vakawanda kuna Mwari. May the Good Lord reward you. Continue to rest in peace.
 Rest in peace our loved Sekuru Munyongani.
I was travelling with Sekuru Munyongani to the Holyland. At the airport he just
disappeared. When he came back he said he had gone to feed his twins.

One of his favourite phrases when he wanted to have a cigarette was "ndiri kuda kumbofida ma twins angu" MHDSRIP.

In November 2015 Israel trip we sang and danced at Zacchaeus Sycamore tree na Sekuru Munyongani. Wow it was wonderful. Please kana paine achine that clip may you post it on this forum and we can celebrate it together. MHDSRIP.

May his dear soul continue to rest in eternal peace.

Thank you, Fr, for allowing us to express ourselves regarding Sekuru we never had the opportunity - not even a memorial service hayo. Inini ndinotenda nomoyo wangu wose.

Haaa sekuru ndinoyeuka Misa yavakatuka vana mbuya Anna kwanzi hamusvodi here kuti nanafata takarasima vana venyu.

Kwai Iwe sis wopfeke bhechu rinosvikokuku moti mvura inaye.

Shinga bhoki mabhonzo anopera nevamwe sekuru vaitidzidzisa kushinga pane zvinorima parish nemumhuri. Tivavarire denga. Sekuru Munyonganani chiedza chisande chikuvhenekerei.

Rimwe zuva vaparidza nyaya yokugarisana zvakanaka, zvikanzi muti wemuvakidzani vakaenda over the durawall ku next door. Uya ndokutema - tema ma branches ose akanga ari divi rokwake ndokukanda zvidimbu zviya na pamusoro pedurawall kuvaridzidzi vomuti. Zvino nyakutema uya akazowachawo nhumbi dzake Ndoku Anika mhepo yakauya ndokutora petticoat yamai ndokupai Kira pedurawall. Uya ndokutora chigero ndoku cheka piece yaive yapfuura muganhu okandawo na pamusoro pe durawall.....

Dzdziso is Inga bude mupfungwa zororai mu rugare rwa Kristo sekuru Munyongani.

Pamusangano waMbuya Anna hanzi vamwe tiri kunamata, vamwe vaakutoshanyira mushana.. Rwendo rwacho runoda manyatera voimba havo.
Many years ago in the U.K. when he was still 'building up ' the Zimbabwe Catholic community , after hearing some unconfirmed reports that we had to be a minimum of 20 for the Chaplain to celebrate mass for us, we rang him to clarify. And his answer clearly was 'the number doesn't matter, even if it's just the two of you I can come'. We will remember him for being always 'there' for everyone! MHDSRIP.
Pfiga musuwo hoyo Satan. A hehe Hallelujah vane moyo yakachena.. Continuing from where I left off.
Tinokuyeukai nguva dzose zvakawanda zvataka dzidza kwamuri. Zororai murugare sekuru .
May his Soul continue to Rest In Peace. Great preacher indeed.
Tatenda zvikuru kuru ndinovimba panopera Covid zvichida tichabatana sezvo mhofu vaifarira zvekuimba toita sponsor music competition in memory of him. Setpiece Mwari ndimi muzere netsitsi. Zvokwadi zvokwadi tinenge taita chinhu chikuru kuru.
Zororai murugare Mhofu yemukono. Basa renyu makaita mukasiya mapedza. Tinotenda Mwari nenguva yava katipa nemi.
Zororai murugare sekuru Munyongani. Upenyu makapedza. Dzidziso makatisiira. Ko tichazodeyi. Penyu makapedza zvasariresu. Ticharamba tichikunamatirayi.
Sekuru Xavier Munyongani, a great man whose sermons were always loaded with relevant humour. Maiwanzoti mutenderi shinga kunamata."Shinga Bhoki mabhonzo anopedzwa navamwe" uye tinofanira kuita reururo nokuti " tose takadya mujozaaaaaa"RIP Mhofu.

Sekuru Munyongani, ndinokutendayi nezvese zvamakatidzidzisa. Zororai murugare. Mutinamatirevererevo. Zororayi murugare Bishop Munyongani muranda waMwari. Sekuru Munyongani, zororai murugare, tinokurangarirai nezvifundiso zvenyu; I.e Kamujoza, tiyeukeiwo. RIP sekuru. He could sing all songs and chorus from other churches. Pane yandakatadza kudeera ndikanzi takuonai Ndimi musingaende kunhamo dzavamwe.

It's amazing to notice how dearly people are holding on videos and pictures about Sekuru Munyongani- Zvimwe tino delita kuitira phone memory izvi zvinenge zvisingadzimiki pamafoni edu- ngatiremekedze mweya wavo nokuita zvakarurama mumunda waTenzi MHSRIP.

Appendix 5: The story (only a part of the story) in pictures

The Person

Bishop Munyongani the priest, bishop, the person. He was everyone's friend.

The Shepherd

Praying 'on the road' with a pilgrim who has asked for a prayer; and celebrating Mass with the faithful. Pilgrims from other countries often asked for prayers and requested him to bless the sacramentals they bought on pilgrimage. Being handed a car bought for him by the Catholic men's Forum in England and Wales soon after his arrival to the UK as Chaplain, a celebratory Mass led by bishop Alan Hopes who was in charge of Ethnic Chaplaincies after Fr Munyongani's elevation to Monsignor.

Shepherding the flock …

Shepherding the flock ...

With Mr Benjamin Takavarasha being inducted into the Guild of The Sacred Heart of Jesus; with Mr and Mrs Mukopfa at the resting place of their young sin Delaine, with the Mukopfas in their home at Leicester, with pilgrims on arrival at Ben Gurion airport, Tel Aviv, Israel; relaxing with a group of his pilgrims; two pilgrims on a different pilgrimage meet Bishop Munyongani in Israel and ask to pose for a photo with him before kneeling for the Bishop's blessing; posing with a group St Anne's Guild members outside The Holy Sepulchre (the Tomb of Jesus at Calvary); relaxing with Joseph Foroma and Samuel Nhavira; gathering outside the house of St Joseph at Nazareth with members of the St Joseph's Guild (which is also next to the Basilica of the Annunciation where the Angel Gabriel brought The Good News to Mary); outside the Church at Cana with Mrs Chimukupete, Mr and Mrs Nhavira, Mrs Mutemachani and others in the background;after a long day on pilgrimage the Bishop and his flock wait for the pilgrimage coach to return to their hotel.arge of Ethnic Chaplaincies after Fr Munyongani's elevation to Monsignor.

On pilgrimage

Jerusalem: Temple Mount and the Tomb of King David
In front of the Dome on Temple Mount, also known as Mount Moriah where Abraham came to offer his only son Isaac as a burnt offering to God; In front of the Tomb of King David. The tomb of David is one of the holiest of Holies within the Jewish Quarter in Jerusalem, and is within the Walls of Jerusalem.

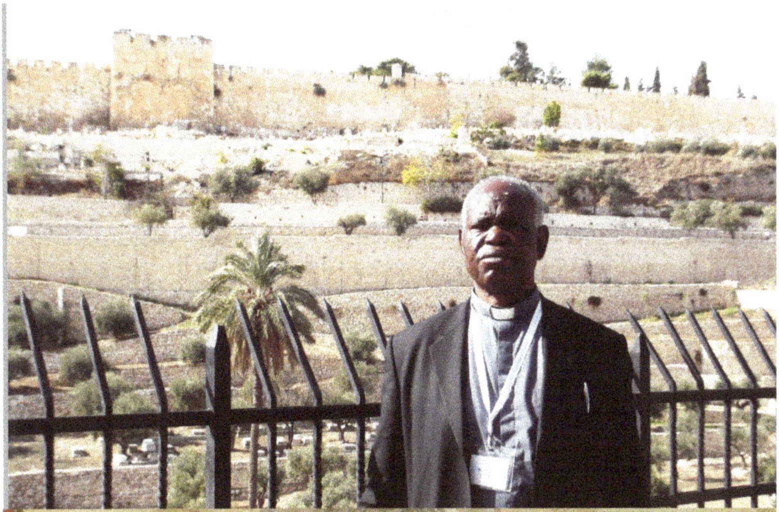

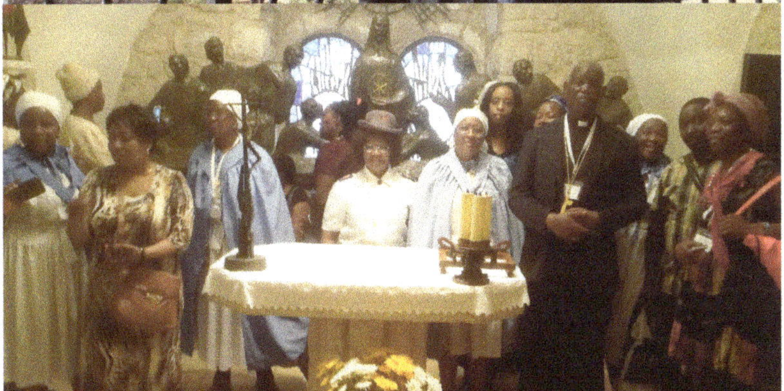

Jerusalem

In the distant background the Walls of the City of Jerusalem, descending on approach into the Kedron Valley; The Upper Room the venue of The Lord's Last Supper; outside the Visitation Church at Ein Kerem (near the birth place of John The Baptist) and the City of Jerusalem in the background as viewed from the Mount of Olives.

Galilee of Nazareth

Outside the Basilica of the Beatitudes; at Cana with couples who have just renewed their wedding vows during Mass; celebrating an open air Mass at the Mount of Beatitudes; the 3 heart shaped rocks representing the number of times Jesus asked Peter "Simon son of Jonah, do you love me?" at The Primacy of St Peter on the shores of the Sea of Galilee. On his last visit to Israel, bishop Munyongani wept uncontrollably during his Mass Homily at this site.

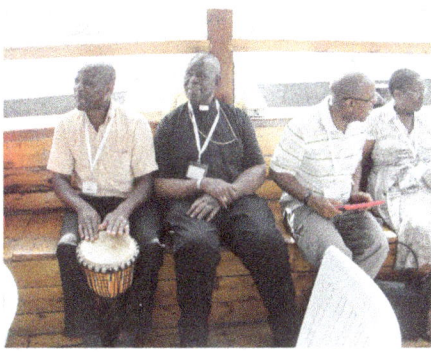 

Boat ride In the Sea of Galilee
Pilgrims and their bishop enjoy the wonderful experience of the boat ride on the Sea of Galilee, the sea on which our Lord Jesus himself often took rides from shore to shore and on which he and Peter walked.

River Jordan site of the Lord's baptism
The Bishop and his pilgrims at the river Jordan, the site of the Lord's baptism by John the Baptist. Baptised pilgrims renew their baptism vows at this pilgrimage site. Seems to be telling them to maintain suitable decorum at this holy site.

Mount of Temptation and at "Zakeyo's" Sycamore tree

In the background the Mount of Temptation where Jesus spent 40 days and 40 nights praying in the wilderness. Bottom right at "Zakeyo's" sycamore tree a short distance away at Jericho.

The Via Dolorosa: Stations of the Cross in Jerusalem - towards Calvary
Bishop Munyongani leads his pilgrims on one of the most solemn parts of their pilgrimage. The walk from Pilate's Praetorium where Jesus was condemned to death and along the route (via Dolorosa) he carried the Cross to his crucifixion at Golgotha on Calvary.

The Holy Sepulchre: The Tomb of Jesus Christ, Jerusalem
The Tomb of Jesus, The Holy Sepulchre, where he was laid to rest after being taken down from the Cross.

Appendix 6: Some special articles from Mr Benjamin Takavarasha's archival collections

[Some parishioners with the Chaplain at the Papal Vigil in Hyde Park on 18 Sept.
Photographer Caroline Khumalo]

Pope Benedict's UK Visit

The Pope's visit from 16 to 19 September was, needless to say, widely reported in the Catholic and secular press, and there is therefore no need to treat the wider aspects of the Pope's visit. That said, we provide a web link to Archbishop Vincent Nichols of Westminster's pastoral letter read in all parishes of the archdiocese on the Sunday immediately following the Pope's visit: http://www.indcatholicnews.com/news.php?viewStory=16792

Our community was directly involved in the historic Papal event to our host country. On Saturday 18 October, the Chaplain recently arrived from Zimbabwe, concelebrated at the Papal mass at Westminster Cathedral. Later on that day, he led his flock to the Papal vigil at Hyde Park in London, and above he is shown with some of his parishioners in the congregation. There was a large contingent of Zimbabweans drawn from those who had been allocated tickets from the quota granted to our community and others who had come via their local parishes. We are grateful to one of our youths, Lorraine Chitanje, for the patience and perseverance to lift the Zimbabwean flag for the greater part of the vigil and the longer period awaiting the Pope's arrival such that it was captured on television. The atmosphere and the Pope's message were indescribable, and many would surely invoke the Pope's predecessor St Peter at Mt Tabor: '*Lord, how good it is that we are here!*' (Mt 17:4)..

The following day September 19 saw another group of Zimbabwean, mainly drawn from our Birmingham community and the rest of the Midlands for the beatification of Cardinal John Henry Newman. Again the Zimbabwean flag was held afloat and captured vividly on National television, and we are grateful to Baba Zenda and Chris Chingwere for patiently holding the flag. Face-to-face and telephone interviews with a random selection of those who attended the event testified to it being a most inspirational event and an occasion to savour in one life time

Since the beatification, the Birmingham Oratory has become a shrine to Bl. Cardinal Henry Newman and a place of pilgrimage, while his statue adorn the front entrance of the Brompton Oratory in South Kensington London. Visit http://www.thepapalvisit.org.uk/Cardinal-Newman.

Installation of the Chaplain as Monsignor

[Section of the crowd at the Installation on 22.08.10. Photographer Mercy Takavarasha]

The installation of Fr Xavier Munyongani as Monsignor in the Papal household took place at Gokomere Mission, Masvingo, on 22 August on the feast of the Patroness to the diocese, Mary Queen of Peace. The open-air mass led by Bishop Michael Bhasera was held with the altar behind the grotto, giving the occasion a visibly Marian flavour. Two days prior to the event, there had been a diocesan convention by the Guild of St Anne (Mbuya Ana), and although it finished on the morning prior to the event, a good number stayed behind who comprised the majority of the congregation which was by and large a sea of green as on the picture above.

While we will focus on the Installation, it was on the whole a multi-pronged event that included the closure of the Year of Priests and the Apostolic blessing of Baba na Mai Machikicho of Silveira Mission. Over their golden wedding anniversary

At the start of the mass, some of us were surprised why he was not at the altar with the other priests, and indeed for a while apparently nowhere to be seen. At the appropriate moment a signal was sent for him to come forward when he headed for the altar. And as a tall figure was approaching the altar, a member of the choir who had been playing the Kudu horn danced and burst into praise poetry for Fr Munyongani's clan:[Shava]:

"**Mhofu yomukono, ziwewera, ziinda nechikaka. mukono waNyashanu**'. And repeated a few times in poetic style. Our inquiries later identified him as Mkwacha, and closely related to the clan and family [mzukuru].

When he was settled at the altar, Bishop Bhasera called on the Vicar General Fr Walter Nytsanza for the evidence upon which he would bestow him the honour, upon which Fr Nyatsanza read the Papal Bull dated 6 February 2010 and also waved it to the congregation. It was announced that on the previous Thursday, Fr Munyongani as then, had celebrated 33 years of the priesthood, and its tempting to place some significance to that hallowed figure! His career was portrayed including 15 years at the Major Seminary in Chishawasha. The Master of ceremony Fr Vincent Muzenda, asked all the priests who had been taught by Fr Munyongani to stand up, and I would say more than 90% of the priests stood up including the MC. Really only a handful of priests were not among them including the Bishop and the most senior priest (chronologically), the veteran Mgr Mavima [Shumba]

After he had been installed, and now in imposing Monsignor regalia (see page 6 col 1), a woman dressed in Mbuya Ana uniform burst from the crowd and was even more unrestrained in her praises and jubilation than Mkwacha as she danced before the altar, perhaps more vividly than King David's dance before the Ark of the Covenant (2 Samuel 6::5).. Our investigation later identified her as the wife of the new Monsignor's elder brother.

The readings (1st: Rev 11: 19A; 12: 1-6A, 10B, 2nd 1 Cor 15: 20—25, Gospel Lk. 1: 39 - 56) were especially chosen to reflect the Marian dimension. In a moving homily by Fr James Munyanyi that encompassed the four themes of the mass, he expounded the fact that the status of Monsignor was not automatically granted on the grounds of age, possibly because the two oldest priests present were indeed elevated to Monsignor! But it was conferred on one's track record.

Cont'd page 6

Shepherding the flock ...

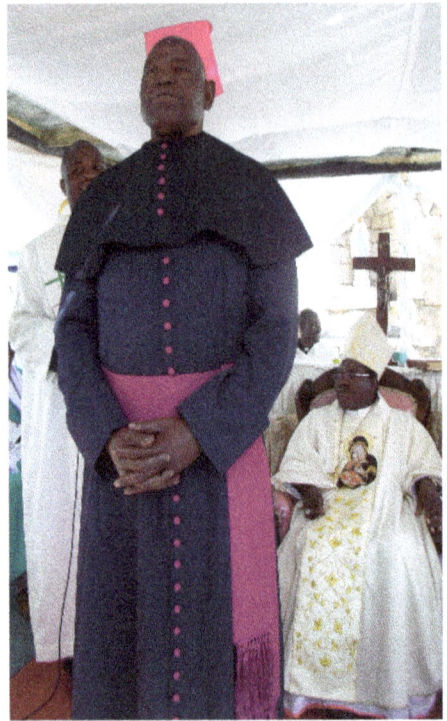

[Recently Installed Monsignor flanked by Bishop Bhasera. Photographer Mercy Takavarasha]

to what the status of Monsignor means, especially as to how it stands vis-à-vis bishopric status. There is hardly any connection between the two and being Monsignor has no hierarchical significance within the Church. It is just an honour just as knighthood in the secular arena here in the UK does not confer executive status beyond what one might already have. Indeed some Monsignors have gone on to be Bishops but still keep their title of Monsignor, but not all bishops are Monsignors, in fact only a tiny minority. What is without doubt, the status carries considerable clout, which but the humility that the homilist expounded, he would walk with his head high, or even walking on water like St Peter on the sea of Galelli?

For the record, one of the most famous Monsignors of all time, perhaps from a secular viewpoint, is Monsignor Georges Lemaître, who, at the Catholic University of Louvain, Belgium, first proposed what in science became known as **the Big Bang theory,** ironically usurped by atheist.

A dvd for the occasion has been produced by **Life Lines** (Dominican Sisters of the Sacred Heart of

He linked the Gospel reading on Mary's humility to say to be elevated to such a status one important ingredient was humility,sSo that God can manifest his power by elevating them (Lk 1:48)

After mass, two speakers sent by our community as delegates to the Installation, the NEC Chair Peter Soko and Mai Mukuru Mai Kapungu were given an opportunity to address the congregation, and although given a very short time, each made brief but moving testimonies on the newly installed Monsignor.

Apart from the two sent by the community, there were a few others from our community who were present including Baba Joseph Foroma, Chair of the London Community and H.E Gabriel Machinga, the Ambassador to London (and his wife), who was also given room to address the congregation..

As far as we are aware, Monsignor Munyongani is only the second Monsignor in Masvingo diocese and only one of very few in the Catholic history of our country. Yet confusion reigns among our Catholic community as

Bishop Munyongani, first priest to be ordained at Mutero

MIRROR REPORTER

MASVINGO – Catholics and non-Catholics alike spoke passionately about the way the late Bishop Xavier Munyongani stood up in defence of the weak.
He was jealous about people's rights whether religious, social or political.
Sekuru Munyongani left tongues wagging at the funeral of Henry Pote where he conducted the Mass a few years ago. He questioned why Pote was not made a national hero when he was the one holding the candle at Enos Nkala's house and taking notes when Zanu PF was formed in 1963. He said there were lesser heroes who made it to national hero status.
In the church he always sang a song which goes 'Vaigara muraini nevamwe zvakanaka.' He urged congregants to respect their neighbours, to live well with their neighbours and to love their neighbours.
Bishop Munyongani came from a small south eastern corner of Gutu that has undoubtedly produced more

priests than any other in Zimbabwe. This area is around Chief Nyamandi and Chitsa's area and its mission is Mutero.

The first person to be ordained priest from the area was Father Ignatious Zvarevashe, a revered author of Shona books. The second person was Munyongani and he was also the first to be ordained at Mutero Mission. Among the servers during his ordination at Mutero was prominent Harare lawyer Ostern Mutero who was only doing Grade 2 then.

The second person to be ordained at Mutero was Peter Marimi who was appointed Vicar General for Gweru Diocese under the late Bishop Francis Mugadzi, There are many others from the famous Mutero area who became priests and they include, McDonald Masvosva who at one time became Vicar General for Masvingo Diocese, Father Gotami, Father Magwidi, Emmanuel Zengeya, Fr Mavedzenge, Fr Mudyiwa, Fr Chaputsira and Father Webster.

Simon Jeffa Mutero, one of the founders of Mutero Mission said Munyongani was one of the most powerful preachers he ever came across. He said there were particularly good sermons like the one he delivered at the ordination of Father Zvarevashe in Mbare in 1979.

"Munyongani was a relative but was also very close to my brother's son Andrew Masvosva who was his classmate at the seminary," said Mutero.

Bishop Munyongani's teacher from Sub A to Standard 3, Philemon Tagutanazvo said Bishop Munyongani was a very obedient boy at school and soft-spoken. He said he was influenced to become a priest by his parents who were devout Catholics.

Bishop Munyongani recently conducted a five hour sermon for his former teacher that kept people captivated, said Tagutanazvo, Local news.
(This article appeared in the Masvingo Mirror at the time of bishop Munyongani's death)

Comment: A letter to the Church in Gweru

This letter is written to you brethren with the full appreciation that it cannot be a pastoral letter – in the mould of the various letters written by St Paul, nor the ones you normally get from the bishops' conference.

I work for a Church media house and the temptation is always to do a PR (public relations) exercise for the Church – turning a blind eye to the faults and putting focus on bright spots so that people see the beauty of our faith. But today, allow me to say a few things in light of the impending consecration of Monsignor Munyongani as your new bishop.

I was amongst you 6 years ago when you welcomed Bishop Munyanyi. There were many people from outside your diocese who came to wish you well. Almost all the members of the ZCBC were there. Even president Mugabe was there. The liturgy was awesome. And more than 6 years later, the majority of Catholics can sing the anthem of that day – *Naisai Gomborereo* – with both pride and nostalgia. The Catholics were one big family –at least on the surface.

It is now a public secret that a small but vocal section of you did not approve of the Pope's appointment then – not because Bishop Martin Munyanyi was not qualified for the job – but because he did not come from Gweru diocese. Sekuru Munyanyi's home area falls outside the boundaries of Gweru diocese, so we were told. Because of this seemingly inconsequential position, the vocal but small section resisted him. Even the ordinary Catholic, who is normally uninterested and unknowledgeable about church politics, became aware of this unfortunate situation.

This is 2013 and Pope Francis has given you a bishop, Monsignor Xavier Munyongani – again a man you will want to say is not from Gweru. He is, strictly speaking, from Masvingo diocese, in Gutu to be particular. But he has worked in Gweru diocese when it was still combined with Masvingo, and he taught almost half the priests who are in the diocese of Gweru today, when they passed through Chishawasha seminary.

I do not know why you put so much emphasis on geography when the issue of one's birthplace is not a major consideration, when one is to be appointed a shepherd in the Church. The Bishop of Rome, Pope Francis is not Roman, neither is he Italian, but hails from a country in South America. Here in Zimbabwe, the archbishop of Harare is not from anywhere in Mashonaland, he is from Hwange. The archbishop of Bulawayo is definitely not from Matabeleland. The bishop of Hwange is Spaniard, and so is Gokwe's bishop Floro. Chinhoyi has a bishop from German. Why should it matter then, when Gweru gets a bishop from outside their diocese?

We all come from different backgrounds, and geographical locations, but we are one family. That is the meaning of the Creed, the faith we profess, that we belong to one apostolic and Catholic Church. Jesus' prayer was that we be one, for He and the Father are one. That is also the meaning of belonging to one body, which is the Church, with one head, who is Christ.

If we profess all these, and still fail to welcome our shepherds, simply because they don't come from our village, then we are fake. We should not be seen reducing our universal Church to a village institution in which leadership options start and end within the circumference of the village itself. I hope you will all unite and pray together with your shepherd, for it is said a family that prays together stays together.

Yours in Christ

Gift Mambipiri

(This article appeared in the Jesuit publication "In Touch" at the time of the episcopal consecration of bishop Munyongani. An article that is so powerful and true to so many other situations in life)

The New Bishop of Gweru

By Benjamin Takavarasha

This Saturday the 14th will see Monsignor Xavier Munyongani installed as the fifth Bishop of Gweru Diocese - after Aloysius Haene, Tobias WungunayiChiginya, Francis Xavier Mugadzi and Martin Munyanyi. He is the first Episcopal appointment in Zimbabwe by Pope Francis when appointed on 15 June. Incidentally and coincidentally his immediate predecessor Bishop Emeritus Martin Munyanyi who retired on ill health was the first Episcopal appointment in Zimbabwe by Pope Benedict XVI on 11 May 2006.

Former Parish Priest, the late Fr John King famously said no one deserves to be a priest in so far as that meant acting in the place of Christ, and we are only there [priests] by the grace of God. If that can be said for a priest, how much more for a Bishop being shepherd to the shepherds as it were.

At the time of his appointment, he was older than all his predecessors at the time of their respective appointments. While some will undoubtedly see this as a downside, it must be remembered that in the history of the Church, many people appointed to high ecclesiastic office in their twilight years still made memorable achievements, to name just two: Henry Cardinal Newman and Blessed John XXIII, who of course spearheaded the Second Vatican Council that revolutionised the Church. Mention can also be made of Pope Francis who reportedly went to the last conclave hoping to tender his resignation largely on the grounds of age. While his Petrine Ministry is still unfolding, probably most Catholics would unequivocally say 'so far so good'.

Monsignor Munyongani will bring a wealth of experience to his Bishopric office apart from his stint as parish priest in a number of parishes in the Old Gweru diocese and Masvingo diocese. From January 1983 to August 1986 he was Novice Master of the newly founded Congregation of St Paul's Brothers in Gweru Diocese; from January 1990 to December 1998, he was teaching Liturgy and Church History at the Major Seminary at Chishawasha, and after a Sabbatical Year in Germany, he resumed teaching Liturgy at the Major Seminary until 2005. In 2006 he managed the Pastoral Centre at Gokomere Mission.

The new Bishop's stint at Chishawasha major Seminary means he will make a head start in that he will know many of his priests from the outset. I remember at his installation as Monsignor at Gokomere on 22 August 2010, the MC Fr Muzenda at one stage asked all the priests who had been taught by Mgr Munyongani to stand up, and I would say more than 90% of the priests stood up. In like manner, he will already know a good percentage of the priests in Gweru Diocese too.

  The new Bishop was appointed whilst Chaplain to the Zimbabwean Catholics in England and Wales, and if reaction from his erstwhile flock is anything to go by, it augurs well for his new challenge whereby the reaction to his appointment has generally been upbeat, and with large attendances at his farewell Masses at the respective 11 centres of the Chaplaincy including the community-wide one in Nottingham on 10 August. The language and tribal mix of Catholics in the Diaspora would surely come in handy in the diverse diocese that Gweru is.

During his five-year stint as Chaplain in England and Wales, there were many innovations that took place, to name but a few: expansion of guilds, introduction of child and youth guilds, the Men's Forum that became a springboard of many joining the St Joseph Guild, the mushrooming of Rosary groups in various localities. However it is not to say he personally initiated those developments but was receptive to good ideas and as such is an enabler. This would come in handy in any diocese but particularly the Gweru Diocese being arguably the most innovative Diocese, albeit as the Old Gweru Diocese, in the history of Catholicism in our country: the pioneer of indigenous Catholic hymns with well known pioneering giants like Stephen Ponde and Simon Mashoko, the birth place of St Anne's guild, now the major guild in four other dioceses, the birth place of the St Joseph Guild, possibly the major Men's guild in each of our eight dioceses, the birth place and home of Moto, the first Catholic Newspaper/Magazine, a major vehicle of Catholic news and also played a pivotal role in our fight for independence, but sadly now defunct for whatever reason. So if Gweru Diocese is not done with its innovative pedigree, it would have a listening ear and an enabler in the new Bishop

No matter how diffident and apprehensive the Bishop-elect could be feeling as the day of destiny approaches, he would take consolation from the adage that God does not call the qualified but qualifies the called. And there is no greater illustration of the latter than the calling of the 12 Apostles as in Tuesday's Gospel, simple fishermen and other workmen (save for the erudite Judas Iscariot – with all the irony that goes with it!) to be the pillars of His Church. Indeed it is a theme so graphically quipped by Pope Benedict XV1 at the very start of his Petrine Ministry when he said he drew consolation and encouragement from working with a Master who is used to using blunt instruments in His vineyard.

Lastly, it is perhaps providential that the Episcopal ordination falls on the feast of the Triumph of the Cross: firstly recognising that the Bishopric office is indeed a Cross but then consoled and encouraged by the fact that the Cross will always triumph. A good omen for the new Bishop?

Update on Shona Pater Noster Plaque in the Holy Land

The project of installing the Pater Noster [the Our Father Prayer] Plaque has been long drawn largely because some aspects of it cannot be hurried and also out of the hand of those who initiated the project. The last two updates on the hallowed project on this Newsletter were in March 2014 (sic:http://shwos.co.uk/Downloads/ZimUKNewsletterMarch2014.pdf, page 3) and in our February 2015 Newsletter.

We are happy to announce that the project has come to a successful end from the latest and last update from the group behind the project, the Gracious Catholic Women (GCW) of our ZCCEW: Here is their report:

Update from Gracious Catholic Women October 2015

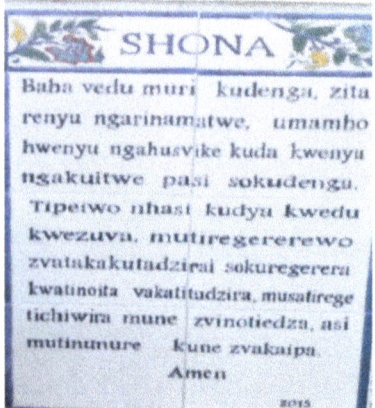

After a long wait, we can now confirm that the plaque has been installed at the Sanctuary of the Eleona at the Pater Noster Church. This is such exciting news and we hope this will make the Holy Land Pilgrimage experience complete spiritually for all Zimbabweans.

The plaque went through verification of Shona prior to approval of its erection. The above is the picture of the plaque and its format although smaller than the first existing plaques in other languages due to limited space at the Sanctuary of the Eleona at the Pater Noster Church. We ask that this message be passed on to all Zimbabwean Catholics including those in Zimbabwe as well as those residing in other countries that we now have a Shona ' Baba Vedu Muri kudenga' prayer plaque in Israel.

On behalf of Gracious Women, I would like to thank everyone for all their support they have given us for this to be successful. It has been one of the biggest challenges, financially and spiritually, but the most satisfying and rewarding.

Gracious Women Chair
Katherine Mutsvangwa

Editor's Note

We can be truly proud and grateful to the Gracious Catholic Women for the successful completion of their project which surely represent one of the major achievements of our ZCCEW and a milestone in Zimbabwean Catholic Community at large.

Our Youth in their inaugural pilgrimage to the Holy Land last August were pleasantly surprised to come across it and a number of photo-calls were made around the plaque some of which we might have occasion to post in future editions.

Happily, the plaque builds up on the one in Ndebele as below that had already been there for some time. We are not privy as to when it was installed nor the circumstances under which it was installed, but whatever the case we are pleased and proud that it is there, especially as it means that our two major vernacular languages are now represented among others across the Christian world

This article (On Page 162) which appeared in the then regular popular community Newsletter ZveSvondo prior to its cessation, covered the progress of the installation of the Shona version of the Lord's Prayer, Our Father alongside more than 100 others in different languages in Jerusalem. The location is the Sanctuary of the Eleona Pater Noster on the Mount of Olives and just a short walk from Gethsemannie. This is where Jesus' disciples asked their Master to teach them to pray and he taught them The Lord's Prayer. This milestone Shona plaque was implemented during the Chaplaincy bishop Munyongani as Chaplain of the Zimbabwean Catholic Community in England and Wales by a group of ladies called the Gracious Catholic Women's Group.

Primacy of St Peter, shore of Sea of Galilee. 3 heart shaped stones signify the 3 times Jesus asked Peter – "Do you love me son of Jonah?" Bishop Munyongani wept there while celebrating Mass on what turned out to be his last visit to the HolyLand. RIP

www.ingramcontent.com/pod-product-compliance
Lightning Source LLC
Chambersburg PA
CBHW040420100526
44589CB00021B/2765